Pride and Prejudice

Jane Austen

Guide written by
John Mahoney

A *Letts* Literature Guide

First published 1994 by BPP (Letts Educational) Ltd,
Aldine House, Aldine Place, London W12 8AW

Text © John Mahoney and Stewart Martin 1994

Typeset by Jordan Publishing Design

Editorial team Rachel Grant, Wayne Davies

Self-test questions devised by Claire Wright

Text design Jonathan Barnard

Cover and text illustrations Hugh Marshall

Graphic illustration Ian Foulis and Associates, Barbara Linton

Design © BPP (Letts Educational) Ltd

British Library Cataloguing in Publication Data
    Martin, Stewart
        Letts Explore 'Pride and Prejudice':
        Letts Educational Literature Guide
        I. Title   II. Mahoney, John
        III. Marshall, Hugh   IV. Foulis, Ian
    823. 7
    ISBN 1 85758 248 9

Printed and bound in Great Britain by
Ashford Colour Press, Gosport, Hants

Contents

■ Plot synopsis

Mr and Mrs Bennet live at Longbourn, Hertfordshire, and have five daughters. Unfortunately, Mr Bennet's estate will not be inherited by his daughters because it is entailed to his cousin, William Collins – a condition of the laws of inheritance. Mrs Bennet is desperate to see her daughters well married to safeguard their future. Mr Collins, a clergyman, has found a living near Rosings, the estate of Lady Catherine de Bourgh.

Charles Bingley, a wealthy bachelor, rents Netherfield, which is an estate near Longbourn. With him are his two sisters and his friend, Fitzwilliam Darcy, who is Lady de Bourgh's nephew.

At a ball, Mr Darcy offends Elizabeth Bennet because of his derogatory remarks about her and her family, whilst Mr Bingley falls in love with Jane, the eldest of the Bennet sisters. Having already had her pride hurt, Elizabeth is willing to believe the lies that a young man, Wickham, tells her about Darcy. In addition, Darcy and the Bingley sisters remove Mr Bingley from the neighbourhood before he has a chance to propose to Jane.

The inane Mr Collins proposes to Elizabeth, but she refuses him. Instead, he marries Elizabeth's friend, Charlotte Lucas. Elizabeth and Darcy meet several times at Rosings, she visiting Charlotte and he his aunt. Darcy falls in love with and proposes to Elizabeth, but in such a proud way that she rejects him and uses the lies spread by Wickham as partial justification for the rejection.

Darcy writes to Elizabeth, defending himself and giving the true background to Wickham's accusations. Elizabeth, in the company of her aunt and uncle, visits Pemberley, Darcy's house, and meets him by chance. His manner towards her is courteous and warm. Elizabeth realises she has misjudged Darcy and that she does love him, but now learns that Lydia, Elizabeth's younger sister, has eloped with Wickham. Darcy intervenes to ensure a marriage takes place and that there is no scandal. Bingley and Jane are reunited, and Darcy and Elizabeth marry. His pride has been humbled, and her prejudice erased.

Characters and themes in *Pride and Prejudice*

The two major characters in the story are Fitzwilliam Darcy and Elizabeth Bennet. Darcy is a wealthy and well-connected man. He is also proud, conscious of social position, the status it confers on him and the obligations he feels it imposes on him. He is shy by nature, which makes his natural pride seem overbearing and insufferable. His sense of social position prejudices his judgement about those of lower social status and this brings him into conflict with Elizabeth Bennet. During the course of the novel, he overcomes his pride and his prejudiced view of Elizabeth and her family.

Elizabeth is witty and intelligent. She is sensitive, and her pride is hurt by the remarks made by Darcy on their first meeting. This leads her to make mistaken judgements about both Wickham and Darcy. Her prejudice blinds her to her growing love for Darcy but she eventually overcomes the prejudice that influenced her judgement of him.

Bingley is a very compliant character. He relies on the judgement of his close friend Darcy and is guided by Darcy's mistaken view of the extent of Jane's affection for Bingley. He is honest, open, friendly and very likeable.

Jane is similar in character to Bingley. Her one fault, if it is a fault, is that she insists on believing the best of everybody.

Mr Bennet is a man who has withdrawn from the world he lives in. Unable to stand the foolishness of his wife, he derives as much amusement as he can from her endeavours to marry off their daughters. He fails in his duties towards his wife and daughters and must take some responsibility for Lydia's elopement.

Mrs Bennet is loud, abrasive and ill-mannered. Her foolishness and lack of intelligence nearly destroy Jane and Elizabeth's chances of finding husbands. However, unlike her husband, her priority – getting her daughters safely married – is practical in terms of securing their future financial security.

Mr Collins is an obnoxious fool. He demonstrates the worst qualities of a self-seeking and insensitive hypocrite.

Love and marriage are the central concerns of the novel. However, Jane Austen is very sceptical of the use of the word 'love' because of the range of different interpretations that people choose to give it. Her ideal relationship is rational as well as emotional, based on mutual esteem, respect, and a clear understanding of the other person's character.

In Mr and Mrs Bennet's relationship we see the long-term results of a marriage based on youthful passion that did not survive the years. Their marriage is balanced by that of their contemporaries, the Gardiners, whose marriage has survived and blossomed and who exemplify the ideal of a happy marriage.

Of the new generation, Lydia and Wickham's marriage is grounded in passion and impulse, and is doomed to be a failure. Charlotte and Mr Collins' marriage is based on mercenary considerations and, whilst likely to last, will not be happy. The choices of Jane and Elizabeth, on the other hand, reflect their desire to find husbands who match them in terms of character and tastes.

The title of the novel describes the other major theme: pride and prejudice. People's pride can easily be hurt and prejudice is quickly built on the slightest of reasons but not so quickly lost. The recognition of one's own faults in these areas and their rectification is a difficult task but can be accomplished if the individual is honest with him- or herself. It is the struggle towards this mutual understanding and self-knowledge that characterises the relationship of Darcy and Elizabeth.

Balance , contrast and structure

Contrasting characters

Elizabeth
lively and teasing
Darcy
serious

Darcy
reserved and haughty
Bingley
agreeable and at ease
with society

Elizabeth
sceptical and perceptive
Jane
accepting and naive

Mrs Bennet
stupid, but concerned
for her daughters
Mr Bennet
intelligent, but not
concerned for his daughters

Darcy
'forbidding, disagreeable'
countenance
Wickham
'amiable' countenance

A troubled relationship

Elizabeth

Darcy

Elizabeth	Darcy
Burdened by her mother	Burdened by his aunt, Lady Catherine
Her sister, Lydia, taken in by Mr Wickham	His sister, Georgiana taken in by Mr Wickham
Generosity and honesty of Mr and Mrs Gardiner and her sister Jane	Charming goodness of Bingley and Colonel Fitzwilliam
Foolishness of her sisters, unctuousness and hypocrisy of her cousin Mr Collins	Sarcasm and spite of the Bingley sisters
To accept Darcy, she must forgive him his opinion of her mother and family	To accept Elizabeth, he must overcome his dislike of her relatives and come to terms with going against the tradition of his heritage

Two balanced halves

FIRST STAGE

SECOND STAGE

Building of pride and prejudice between Elizabeth and Darcy

Darcy and Bingley at Netherfield Hall

Marriage of Charlotte and Mr Collins

Elizabeth makes a journey to Hunsford in Kent and meets Mr Darcy

Darcy proposes to Elizabeth

Elizabeth crosses Lady Catherine

Breaking down of pride and prejudice between Elizabeth and Darcy

Darcy and Elizabeth to marry

Darcy and Bingley at Netherfield Hall

Elizabeth crosses Lady Catherine

Marriage of Wickham and Lydia

Elizabeth makes a journey to Pemberley and meets Darcy

Some important letters

Darcy's letter to Elizabeth begins her change of heart, and reveals the beginnings of change in Darcy's unbending character

Jane's two letters to Elizabeth create suspense and recount the elopement of Lydia, making Elizabeth feel all hopes of a relationship with Darcy are destroyed

Mrs Gardiner's letter to Elizabeth illuminates Darcy's generosity and good character

Mr Collins' letters to the Bennets disclose his self-centred and hypocritical nature

Lydia's letters show the irresponsibility and selfishness of her character

Elizabeth Bennet

Elizabeth, the second of the Bennet daughters and her father's favourite, is the heroine of the novel. She is intelligent, lively, witty and quite capable of holding her own in conversation with someone as well educated as Darcy. She is a strong character with sufficient belief in herself to stand up to such figures as Mr Collins, Lady Catherine de Bourgh and Darcy. She is deeply affectionate, as witnessed by the sorrow she feels for Jane, whose compassionate nature she much admires. She is perceptive, which helps her to assess accurately the characters of Bingley, his sister and Lady Catherine, but is wrong when she judges Wickham and Darcy. Completely taken in by appearances, she unquestioningly accepts all that Wickham says. She is proud, however, and it is her hurt pride that first makes her prejudiced against Darcy. It is her pride, too, that is flattered by Wickham, who singles her out for personal attention. It is this mixture of pride and prejudice that blunts her judgement of the two men.

Elizabeth reveals a maturity and wisdom beyond that of her parents. She censures her father for not acting responsibly towards his children. She finds irksome her mother's preoccupation with trivia. The atmosphere at home is too confining for her spirits. Above all else, it is Elizabeth's teasing, impulsive disposition which makes her so appealing: Darcy says near the end of the novel that it was the 'liveliness' of her mind that first attracted him.

Jane Bennet

Jane is the eldest and the most beautiful of the Bennet girls. She is so sweet-natured that her desire to find good in everyone is almost a fault. This leads her to be undiscerning in her assessment of character sometimes. For a long time she refuses to believe that Miss Bingley is hypocritical. She tries to see virtue in both Wickham and Darcy at the same time. She is an excellent foil for Elizabeth, causing the latter to re-think and justify her often hasty conclusions about people. Their affectionate relationship is one of the most pleasing aspects of the book. Jane keeps her own feelings hidden and while this helps her to cope when Bingley suddenly leaves the area, it does also lead Darcy into believing that she does not care much for Bingley. Jane, although a pleasant character, is naive.

Mr Darcy

Mr Darcy's character is difficult to assess because he is seen almost entirely through Elizabeth's eyes. Therefore it is necessary to look behind her prejudice to find the true man. Certainly he is proud and unnecessarily rude about Elizabeth when they first meet, but it gradually becomes apparent to the reader that his first impressions of her were wrong and he becomes increasingly attracted to her. He attributes his haughtiness and social unease to shyness: 'We neither of us perform well to strangers', he says to Elizabeth. Shy or not, he is intolerant of other people. Unlike Bingley, who is his opposite in character, he finds Mrs Bennet's behaviour vulgar and embarrassing. He considers Elizabeth's inferior background an impediment to their relationship, even whilst he is proposing to her. He has a cutting wit which puts people in their place when he feels they have overstepped the bounds of decorum. Both Miss Bingley and Sir William Lucas feel the edge of his tongue.

Darcy's good qualities remain hidden until Elizabeth goes to Pemberley. There she learns from the housekeeper what a fine master, landlord and brother he is. He in his turn, chastened by Elizabeth's rebuff at Hunsford, modifies his behaviour in recognition of her criticisms of his pride, arrogance and snobbery. The full extent of Darcy's good nature is seen in his generosity and sense of responsibility towards Lydia and Wickham, prompted as he is by his feelings for Elizabeth. Although a humbler person at the end of the novel, he remains serious. Elizabeth knows that he still is not ready to be teased, although she has every intention of making him less serious with her 'lively, sportive manner of talking'.

Mr Bingley

Charles Bingley is a rich, handsome, eligible young man who rents a house three miles away from Longbourn. He is sociable, uncomplicated and agreeable. Unlike his sisters and his friend Darcy, he is not offended by the Bennet family's lack of breeding. He is very attracted to Jane but, being of a compliant disposition, he is easily persuaded by his sisters and his friend Darcy to leave the neighbourhood and return to London. It is only when the relationship between Darcy and Elizabeth is resolved that he and Jane are finally brought together.

Mr and Mrs Bennet

Mr Bennet is an intelligent, witty man who nevertheless fails in his duty as a father. Disillusioned by an unhappy marriage, he retreats from his family, in a physical sense by taking refuge in his library and in a moral sense by refusing to take his responsibility as a parent seriously. Instead of guiding and teaching his daughters, he teases and mocks them. Although he is shocked and chastened by Lydia's elopement, his character does not really change. He reverts to his lazy and selfish life once the crisis is over.

Mrs Bennet is a woman of little understanding or intelligence. She is insensitive to the feelings of others, superficial in thought, and loud in speech. She embarrasses her husband and Elizabeth. Her main occupation is arranging for her five daughters to be married to wealthy husbands. This desire dominates her life.

She is a woman of superficial feeling, quickly irritated and equally rapidly calmed. Her opinion of Darcy changes immediately on hearing that he is to marry Elizabeth. She is childish in her judgement of people, blaming Mr Collins for the entailment on the Bennet property, and Bingley for Jane's unhappiness. She is the butt of her husband's sarcasm. Ironically, her lack of breeding and thoughtlessness almost prevent Jane and Elizabeth from making the satisfactory matches she so much desires for them.

Mr Collins

Mr Collins is pompous, insensitive and foolish, and is the object of great satire in the novel. Obsequious to Lady Catherine, he is not perceptive enough to see that she is overbearingly patronising. His lack of self-knowledge and his uncritical mind mean that he does not understand why Elizabeth rejects him. Although his pride is hurt by the rejection, his feelings are shown to be shallow when he proposes to Charlotte Lucas almost immediately afterwards. His materialistic outlook on life, which makes him value the quantity or size of houses and furnishings while totally ignoring their aesthetic qualities, ill befits a clergyman. His lack of Christian spirit is revealed in the letter he writes to the Bennets after Lydia's marriage.

Lydia Bennet

Lydia is the youngest Bennet daughter and the first to be married, as she proudly announces. Very much like her mother she is self-centred, frivolous and superficial, interested only in clothes, dances and the neighbouring officers. She is shameless about her behaviour with Wickham and quite unaware of the anxiety and trouble she has caused her family. She is unfeeling and tactless, especially to her sisters after her marriage. Elizabeth is very critical of her, considering her 'ignorant, idle and vain'.

Caroline Bingley

Miss Bingley is rich, proud and very aware of her social position. She scorns the Bennet family for their lack of sophistication and because they have relations in 'trade'. The irony is that it is this source that created her own inherited wealth. Although superficially civil, she despises Elizabeth in particular, as she is jealous of the attention that Darcy pays her. Miss Bingley speaks spitefully and sarcastically about Elizabeth in a vain attempt to gain Darcy's interest in herself. Although one may feel sorry that she is unable to attract the man she wants, she nonetheless remains a hypocrite and a snob.

Lady Catherine de Bourgh

Lady Catherine has an overdeveloped sense of her own importance. She feels that her rank as a lady gives her the right to offer opinions to anyone and everyone on any subject at all. She is not in the habit of being contradicted, surrounded as she is by flatterers like Mr Collins. Her habit of speaking her mind is often an excuse for incivility, and she is so used to having her own way that she is completely taken by surprise when Elizabeth refuses to promise her not to marry Darcy.

Charlotte Lucas

Charlotte, Elizabeth's friend, is a realist. Aware of her poor financial status, she is prepared to marry solely for economic reasons. Although this shocks Elizabeth, there were very few options for a woman in her position in that society. Having made the decision to become mistress of Hunsford, Mr Collins' home, she carries out her duties correctly and amiably and seems happy. She is sensible to realise that she must keep on good terms with Lady Catherine and pays the necessary courtesy visits, avoiding confrontation. She cleverly reorganises the rooms at Hunsford to ensure that she sees little of Mr Collins during the day!

George Wickham

George Wickham is an officer in the regiment stationed at Meryton, near Longbourn. He is an attractive figure who deceives Elizabeth, her family and the neighbourhood into thinking he is a worthy character. His story about the injustice he suffered at the hands of Darcy is sufficient to draw everyone's sympathy and it is accepted uncritically. Elizabeth even excuses him when, for purely mercenary reasons, he transfers his attentions from her to Miss King. His true character is revealed by Darcy only under pressure. Wickham is a spendthrift, a liar and a womaniser. He is persuaded to marry Lydia, and so prevent a dreadful scandal, only by being given a great sum of money.

Themes in *Pride and Prejudice*

Love and marriage

Love and marriage

Although this book is chiefly concerned with marriage, Austen does not often use the word love. When she does, she is sceptical of its meaning. The phrase 'violently in love' is described as 'hackneyed, doubtful and indefinite' (Chapter 25). To her it can mean anything from a short acquaintance to a 'strong attachment'. She is uncertain of the lasting qualities of passionate love, and convinced that it is not a strong enough basis for marriage. True love is rational as well as emotional. It is based on mutual esteem, respect and gratitude, and it arises from a clear-sighted understanding of the other person's character. Passion is part of it, but must be controlled. True love has the power to change people: Elizabeth attributes Darcy's loss of pride to 'love, ardent love'. It also has the power to persuade people. Conscious of Darcy's regard for her, Elizabeth grows to love him partly through gratitude for his love.

Austen is interested in the way people select their partners and the main theme of the novel is marriage. In *Pride and Prejudice* there are four weddings so there is plenty of scope to explore this theme. Austen describes three different kinds of marriage. There is the mercenary marriage brought about entirely for economic reasons. The union between Charlotte and Mr Collins is a good example of this. Charlotte is pessimistic about finding happiness in marriage anyway, and believes she may as well marry to guarantee her financial security. For a woman without personal fortune, this was an attractive basis for marriage.

Almost completely in contrast to this prudent view is the marriage based solely on passion and physical attraction. Lydia and Wickham make such a marriage, as did Mr and Mrs Bennet years before. The success of such a union can be judged by looking at the relationship between Mr and Mrs Bennet. Once the excitement of 'youth and beauty' had faded, the two people found they did not understand or even like each other. Given the character of Wickham, it should not seem strange that he held out for as good an economic settlement as possible before agreeing to marry Lydia, but the initial attraction between the two had everything to do with passion and physical attraction and little to do with mutual understanding of character.

Somewhere in between these two views of marriage lies the ideal. It is characterised by the relationships between Darcy and Elizabeth, and between Jane and Bingley. Whilst the characters of the two sets of people are very different, these relationships are 'rationally founded', based on 'excellent understanding' and 'general similarity of feeling and taste' (Ch 55). Austen believes that in relationships, reason should dominate emotion. Both partners must have compatibility of interests, temperament and intelligence for a marriage to work well.

Austen lived in a mercenary world and this is reflected in the novel. No secret is made of the need to marry for money. A woman who has no fortune must look for a man who has, and vice versa – something which even Elizabeth admits. She criticises Charlotte, not for marrying a wealthy man, but for marrying solely for money. On the other hand, she quite accepts Wickham's motives for transferring his attentions from herself to Miss King, a rich woman. Mrs Bennet's fixation with marriage can be largely explained by the poor financial position of her daughters. Nevertheless, Austen would be the last to deny the important part money played in the society she describes. Were it not for the generosity of Darcy in settling a large sum of money on Wickham, thereby averting the scandal if no marriage had taken place, none of the Bennet girls would have stood much chance of marrying.

Pride and prejudice

Pride and prejudice

It is frequently difficult to separate cause and effect with regard to this major theme. Darcy's pride in his family, social class and connections lead him to be prejudiced against people of Elizabeth's (comparatively lesser) social standing. His arrogant treatment of Elizabeth offends *her* innate pride and, in turn, prejudices her against him.

The novel examines the nature of pride. Darcy is censured for his pride by public opinion in general and by

Elizabeth in particular. This disapproval is deserved, as his uncivil behaviour at the Netherfield ball offends the etiquette of the time, although Charlotte Lucas thought his social rank gave him the right to haughty manners.

Darcy himself attributes his lack of ease to shyness, not pride, but he does admit to the fault of snobbery: he is prejudiced against Elizabeth's social inferiority. Elizabeth, too, is guilty of pride: her prejudice against Darcy initally arose primarily from hurt pride. She takes an immediate dislike to Darcy because of his supercilious attitude, and because he hurts her pride with his insensitive remarks about her looks. Prejudiced against Darcy, she is easily deceived by Wickham because she wants to believe badly of Darcy. It is interesting to compare how she views Darcy before and after she discovers the truth of his character. Before receiving the letter which changes everything, she can see no further than his pride: 'his abominable pride'. At Pemberley, after the revelations of his letter, she is 'amazed at the alteration in his manner', an alteration due partly to less pride on his part but also to less prejudice on hers.

Aspects of society

Austen was writing in the early nineteenth century (*Pride and Prejudice* was first published in 1813) about the landed gentry of England – people whose wealth was inherited, having been generated by the world-wide trading activities of their ancestors. She was concerned almost entirely with the way this section of society behaved. These people enjoyed a comfortable, leisurely life, enjoying the gaiety of London society in the winter and returning to their country residences in the summer. Austen describes their attitudes, social behaviour and preoccupations in detail. They form a tight-knit group, bound by strict codes of conduct, often snobbish and mercenary, as well as censorious of those who contravene their social and moral standards. Within this society, strict etiquette governs such matters as introducing oneself as, or to, a new neighbour. The way people behave therefore qualifies or disqualifies them as members of this social group. The word Jane Austen most frequently uses in this context is 'civility'. A thorough understanding of the way this society operates is essential if the reader is to appreciate and understand Austen's novel.

■ Text commentary

Chapter 1

The arrival of Mr Bingley at Netherfield Park is keenly anticipated by Mrs Bennet, whose main purpose in life is to see her five daughters successfully married. Her husband does not share her excitement and appears reluctant to introduce himself to Mr Bingley. He demonstrates a distinct lack of interest in family affairs.

Marital affairs

Love and marriage

In the opening sentence Austen sums up the theme of her book. She is being ironic, implying that very often parents with daughters assume that single men of 'good fortune' want to get married, when in fact it may be the last thing they want.

In this first chapter we are introduced to Mr and Mrs Bennet and quickly, through dialogue, we have a good idea of their characters, and their marriage. Look at the way Mr Bennet teases his wife: he knows Mr Bingley's arrival is of great importance to his daughters' marital expectations, yet he pretends to be disinterested. He does not appear to share his wife's preoccupations: for Mrs Bennet the matter of making social contact with all eligible bachelors is a very serious one; Mr Bennet makes light of it, mocking her seriousness and teasing her.

The characters of Mr and Mrs Bennet are summed up in the last paragraph of the chapter. Their marriage cannot have been close, if twenty-three years has been 'insufficient to make his wife understand his character'.

Manners

Notice the strict code of behaviour at this time. It would have seemed discourteous for women to visit a new neighbour without previous formal introduction by the head of the household. Mr Bennet has to visit Mr Bingley and introduce himself before any social contact between the two families can take place.

Chapter 2

Mr Bennet enjoys teasing his family by keeping them ignorant of his visit to Netherfield

Hall. Mrs Bennet is irritated by this hitch in her plans, but her mood soon turns to joy when Mr Bennet reveals that he has visited Mr Bingley.

Mr Bennet enjoys himself

Mr Bennet is very sarcastic about his youngest daughters Kitty and Mary, and again mocks his wife. It seems that he derives much enjoyment from teasing his wife, and has a low opinion of certain of his daughters. The fact that he has to derive pleasure from his family in this way suggests that he is not very happily married and that, really, he is disaffected with his family life.

An 'uncertain temper'

Notice how irritable Mrs Bennet becomes when she thinks her plans are going to be frustrated by her husband's refusal to pay a call on Bingley. Moments later, she has a complete change of mood on hearing the good news that he *has* visited Mr Bingley. This is a good example of her 'uncertain temper', described by Austen at the end of the previous chapter.

Mary and Lydia

The most serious of the five Bennet girls, Mary derives wisdom from reading books. Unlike her father and her sister Elizabeth, she lacks the perception to judge people by their behaviour, so her pronouncements, when she makes them, sound empty and irrelevant. Look at Chapters 5 and 47 for examples of this. We are immediately made aware of Lydia's self-confidence and lack of sense – she thinks her height will make up for her lack of maturity!

Chapter 3

Mr Bingley returns Mr Bennet's visit, but the ladies, only glimpsing him, have to be content with second-hand information, until they go to the ball he holds at Netherfield Hall. Here the general opinion that Mr Bingley is agreeable and handsome is confirmed but, in contrast, his friend Mr Darcy is found to be proud and unfriendly. He deeply offends Mrs Bennet by slighting Elizabeth, but she, unlike her mother, does not take his comments to heart. Mrs Bennet is gratified that Jane seems to have made a good impression on Mr Bingley.

> Austen is ironic about the assumptions made by society: 'To be fond of dancing was a certain step towards falling in love'. Yet there is truth in her statement: within the context of that society, the dance was the only way that two people could have a private conversation in public. Look at Chapter 18 to see how Elizabeth and Darcy make use of this social convention. Notice how, at the ball, the newcomers are described through the eyes of all the people present. In this way, Austen emphasises the fact that the individual is a part of society, answerable to others as much as to him- or herself.

Mrs Bennet's aim in life

Love and marriage

The aim of Mrs Bennet's life is summarised at the beginning of Chapter 3: 'If I can but see one of my daughters happily settled…'. In this respect she seems to be more aware of her duties as a parent than her husband. Where she falls down is in her failure to appreciate the dangers of finding an unsuitable partner – something her own marriage should have taught her. For her, a 'suitable' husband is a wealthy one.

Darcy exhibits his pride

Jane Austen satirises public opinion here. The rumour of Mr Darcy's wealth

Mr Darcy

is taken as fact, and his character is judged by his appearance: a 'forbidding, disagreeable countenance'. The general opinion is quickly formed about Mr Darcy. 'His character was decided' on the strength of his unsociable behaviour. Heightened by contrast with Bingley's amiable behaviour, Darcy's arrogance is condemned, and prejudice against him sets in. The dialogue in this chapter quite forcefully reveals Darcy's pride. Later he maintains it was shyness that led to his awkward behaviour at the ball. However, it is hard to justify his comments on such grounds, especially in the remarks he makes about Elizabeth. Later, when he first proposes to her, his attitude is just as proud, but there he explains his reasons for such offensive behaviour: 'His sense of her inferiority…of the family obstacles…were dwelt on'.

Elizabeth's pride is hurt

The society Austen describes was very quick to judge on appearances. Just as Darcy had been judged by the assembly, so Elizabeth quickly makes up her mind. Her reaction to his insult, making a joke of it to her family and friends, shows that she is resilient and lively.

Chapter 4

This chapter involves the four main characters of the book. Jane and Elizabeth are contrasted, as are Bingley and Darcy. Jane reveals a kind, uncritical nature, ready to see only good in people. Elizabeth is more intelligent, more observant, and more critical of people's hypocrisy. She is less impressed than Jane by Bingley's sisters. They have had all the upbringing and privileges of ladies and should therefore act as such, but Elizabeth does not think they do. Bingley and Darcy are presented as opposites: the former is less clever, but more agreeable and sociable than Darcy, who is 'haughty and reserved'. Their opinions of the ball are very different.

A difference of perception

Jane is shown to accept people at face value. She is impressed with Bingley

because of his good breeding and manners. Elizabeth mocks her a little when she says: 'His character is thereby complete'. She feels that judgement should be more discerning, and yet it is she, not Jane, who is later guilty of being deceived by appearances – note her ready acceptance of Wickham later in the book. Elizabeth draws attention to Jane's kind nature, but Jane's ability to see good in everyone affects her judgement. Her view that Miss Bingley is 'charming' is not shared by Elizabeth. As we get to know Miss Bingley better, it is obvious that Elizabeth's 'quickness of observation' has given her a truer assessment of Miss Bingley's character – again, that faculty will be less obvious when it comes to judging Wickham's character.

Manners and breeding

Manners and breeding were of considerable importance in upper-class circles. They play a major role in the novel as it is the Bennet family's lack of breeding that is a major impediment to the progress of Elizabeth and Darcy's relationship. To belong to a family whose fortune was made in trade was to belong to an inferior class. It is ironic to see Miss Bingley's disdain for the Bennet family because they have relations in 'trade'. In that society, Miss Bingley and her sister should have been called 'ladies' as they fulfil all the requirements: they have money, beauty and are accompished. but although Elizabeth notes, with irony, that they were: 'in every respect entitled to think well of themselves…', their subsequent behaviour, particularly with regard to the Bennets, is far from 'ladylike'. 'Manners' are a better indication of 'breeding' than is birth: contrast Lady de Bourgh and Mrs Gardiner.

Opposites in character, but friends

In this chapter Darcy and Bingley are compared. The two men are described as being quite opposite in temperament: Bingley is easy-going and sociable; Darcy is complicated and distant. Of the two, Darcy is the more intelligent and Bingley respects his judgement. To illustrate this contrast, their impressions of the ball are very different.

Chapter 5

The Bennets discuss the ball with their friends, the Lucases. Mrs Bennet is delighted with Jane's success at having danced twice with Bingley. Everyone except Jane is agreed that Darcy's character is quite unpleasant and that his pride is overbearing. Only Charlotte Lucas feels that his social rank gives him the right to be proud.

Austen uses satire to describe Sir William Lucas' new position as a gentleman. In a society clearly divided by rank, he regards it as important to sever all connection with his past life as a businessman. Although Elizabeth mocks him gently, he is not an unpleasant character.

Darcy's pride excused?

Mr Darcy

It is left to Jane to find something good to say about Darcy. She is the only one to suggest that his reserve is due more to shyness than pride. This is the reason he gives for his behaviour later in the novel, and when we meet his sister, she too is very shy in company. Charlotte Lucas' suggestion that Darcy's rank justifies his pride tells us a little about her attitude to men of fortune. This in turn prepares us for her response when Mr Collins proposes.

Chapter 6

The acquaintance between the Bennets and the Bingley sisters grows and although the latter admit to liking Jane and Elizabeth, the rest of the family are found to be 'intolerable'. Elizabeth's liking for them, however, does not grow. Charlotte Lucas warns that Jane must make her feelings clear if she wishes to encourage Bingley. Her rather scheming, cynical view of marriage, where a woman may as well marry for money as for love, as 'Happiness in marriage is entirely a matter of chance', contradicts Elizabeth's view that a happy marriage must be based on mutual knowledge and understanding. Elizabeth becomes aware that Darcy is taking a keener interest in her. Through pride she refuses to dance with him, as she assumes he is merely being polite. Miss Bingley is surprised that Darcy seems to have changed his opinion of Elizabeth, and is immediately jealous.

A discussion of marriage and love

Jane Bennet

Charlotte's remark that Jane 'may lose the opportunity of fixing' Bingley because of her 'composure of temper and uniform cheerfulness', is proved correct later in the novel. Look at Chapter 35 to see that this is exactly the reason Darcy gives for believing that Jane had no special affection for Bingley. This is an excellent example of the care Austen takes to construct a plot in which every comment is significant and every character plays an intrinsic role. Charlotte is more worldly than Jane, and is aware of the importance of appearance in a society which lays so much stress on behaviour.

Charlotte's views on marriage are very different from Elizabeth's. In marrying, Charlotte is chiefly concerned with obtaining a good financial match: sentiment plays little part. Elizabeth, on the other hand, feels that marriage should be a union based on mutual knowledge and understanding.

Love and marriage

She protests that Jane does not yet know Bingley well enough to have decided whether she is in love with him or not.

'Happiness in marriage is entirely a matter of chance.' Charlotte makes it clear that she sees marriage in terms of economics. Her expectations are no higher than that. Again, note the way that Austen prepares us for future events. Knowing her views, we should not be surprised when Charlotte accepts Mr Collins' proposal. Elizabeth does not think that Charlotte, with her cynical view of marriage, is being serious. Notice the dramatic irony in her comment: 'You would never act in this way yourself!' – again, Elizabeth's judgement will prove unsound.

Elizabeth asserts her independence

Darcy, whilst maintaining that Elizabeth's manners are 'not those of the fashionable world', is nevertheless attracted by her 'playfulness'. Unbeknown to her, his interest in her is increasing.

As if understanding his thoughts, Elizabeth shows the 'playfulness' of her character in their dialogue. She is lively and teasing towards him, determined to use the weapon of her wit to face his 'satirical eye'. But Elizabeth, too, has her pride, and she will not let it be thought that she was hunting for a partner (this is her fear later in the novel, when she meets Darcy by chance at Pemberley). However, by refusing to dance with Darcy, she only increases her attractiveness. He sees spirit and pride in her character, an independence of mind which appeals to him.

Darcy finds himself attracted

Miss Bingley expresses contempt at the dullness of the society before her. These people talk of nothing yet create much noise: the conversation between Sir William and Darcy and the musical recital justify her complaint. However, her contempt is also occasioned by jealousy. Darcy has changed his opinion of Elizabeth: before, he thought her merely 'tolerable'; now, he thinks she has 'a pair of fine eyes' and is 'pretty'.

Caroline Bingley is surprised when Darcy contradicts her opinions. Her jealousy is expressed in sarcasm: 'pray when am I to wish you joy?' Yet she brings up an important issue when she mentions Mrs Bennet. Although Darcy does not show it, he is concerned about Mrs Bennet's lack of social grace.

> All the main characters have been introduced.
>
> The theme of **marriage** has been well aired, particularly in Mrs Bennet's drive to get her daughters married.
>
> Relationships between **Jane** and **Bingley**, and **Elizabeth** and **Darcy** have begun.
>
> The **pride and prejudice** of both Darcy and Elizabeth is a barrier to the development of their relationship.

Chapter 7

Mrs Bennet's eagerness to see her daughters married is explained. Mr Bennet's estate will not be left to them on his death, and so for economic reasons they need to marry well. The younger daughters are delighted at the arrival of a militia regiment in Meryton and Mrs Bennet approves of their association with the officers. Jane receives an invitation to dine at Netherfield and Mrs Bennet works out a ruse to enable Jane to spend the night there. The plan goes amiss as Jane becomes ill and has to stay there while she recovers. Elizabeth goes to look after her. Thus Austen brings the four main characters together and the plot can be progressed further.

The information about the entail is important as it explains Mrs Bennet's near obsession with obtaining wealthy husbands for her daughters. Her concern is mainly economic. Because none of them will inherit their father's estate, marrying well is the only way to safeguard against future poverty.

Love and marriage

Like mother, like daughter

The two girls, Catherine (Kitty) and Lydia seem very impressed with superficial appearances such as the 'regimentals of an ensign', proving the earlier observation that: 'their minds were more vacant than their sister' (Ch 7). Their father is contemptuous of their chatter but their attitudes towards him are different. It is significant that while Catherine takes heed of what he says, Lydia totally ignores him. Lydia and Catherine's future actions reflect this difference in character.

Foolish Mrs Bennet

Mr Bennet is again ironic in his conversation with his wife. In almost no respect do they agree and again he has fun at her expense. Her lack of perception and decorum is evident in the way she defends Lydia. Despite her lack of intelligence, she has the guile to formulate a scheme to keep Jane at Netherfield overnight. However, her foolishness surfaces when she smugly praises herself for the success of the idea, showing no regard for the danger to her daughter's health by being caught in the rain.

Elizabeth shows her spirit

Elizabeth's independence of spirit is again shown by her decision to walk to Netherfield in order to visit her sister. The effect of the walk on her complexion is not lost on Darcy, although the Bingley sisters are horrified at such unorthodox behaviour.

Chapter 8

The Bingley sisters' concern for Jane is shown to be superficial. They are also critical of Elizabeth's appearance and behaviour when she is out of the room, and are scornful of the Bennets' social rank. Miss Bingley attempts to impress Darcy with compliments and praise, but it is Elizabeth's intelligence and independence of thought which he notices. Jane's health continues to give cause for concern.

Notice the importance of family status and background when choosing a partner for marriage and how different Bingley and Darcy's views are on the subject. Bingley's kind nature contrasts with his sisters' spitefulness, and he tries to soften the sharpness of Miss Bingley's words with sympathetic remarks of his own.

Bingley's description of 'accomplished' women gives an insight into the kinds of activities upper-class women undertook at that time. Theirs was a gentle, delicate existence, and Elizabeth's behaviour, walking (through mud) to Netherfield would not have been considered ladylike. We can sense, though, Austen's humour at the kind of 'accomplishments' the Bingleys describe. Elizabeth's physical and mental energy is, we feel, condoned by the author.

Chapter 9

Mrs Bennet arrives to see Jane. Having assured herself of Jane's recovery, she is happy to converse with the occupants of Netherfield. Much to the discomfort of Elizabeth, she shows herself to be inquisitive, insulting, shallow, and narrow-minded. Elizabeth, in contrast, is witty and intelligent and impresses Darcy further. He is left with the problem of liking the daughter but scorning her mother. Mr Bingley promises Lydia that he will hold a ball when Jane is better.

Civility and breeding

The oil that lubricated the social intercourse of this class of people was 'civility'. Even Miss Bingley, who has no respect whatsoever for Mrs Bennet, manages to speak to her with 'cold' civility. Look back to the way Darcy spoke of Elizabeth on first seeing her (Chapter 3). That is why he was so severely censured by public opinion: he lacked 'civility'.

Mr and Mrs Bennet

Mrs Bennet's lack of breeding is apparent when she quizzes Bingley on his intentions to leave or stay at Netherfield. Then she reveals her hostility towards Darcy and makes herself look foolish by misunderstanding his comment about country people. Elizabeth, 'blushing for her mother', tries to change the subject.

Country dullards?

There is an underlying assumption that country life and country people are

Pride and prejudice

dull. Look back at Darcy's boredom with the evening's entertainment (Chapter 6). This prejudice against country people explains his comment (Chapter 32) to Elizabeth: '*You* cannot have been always at Longbourn'. As if to confirm Darcy's feelings about the narrowness of country life, Mrs Bennet boasts in a childish, unintelligent way about the number of families in the Bennet's social circle. Her remark about 'those people who fancy themselves...' is a very thinly disguised criticism of the present company.

Darcy warms to Elizabeth

Mr Darcy

Darcy cannot help but be impressed with Elizabeth's wit. She is forced to try and lighten the awkward atmosphere created by her mother's boastful and tactless conversation. In the final sentence of this chapter we learn that Darcy will not join the others in criticising Elizabeth.

Chapter 10

Miss Bingley flatters and compliments Darcy, but gets little response. Mr Bingley, Mr Darcy and Elizabeth engage in a discussion about Bingley's readiness to agree with his friends. Mr Darcy and Elizabeth match each other in intelligence and witty repartee. Darcy's interest in Elizabeth grows but she, still prejudiced against him, senses only disapproval in his manner towards her. Miss Bingley, prompted by jealousy of Elizabeth, is very spiteful and sarcastic about the Bennet family.

Contrasting characters: Bingley and Darcy

Mr Darcy

Mr Bingley

The contrast between Darcy and Bingley is again highlighted by the description of their different styles of writing. Letters form an important part of the novel. One of their chief uses is to reveal character. Darcy's measured style of writing reflects his staid, proud character. Bingley's more careless style of writing is in keeping with his agreeable and impulsive nature.

When Darcy and Bingley discuss the pliancy of Bingley's character, we should be aware of the careful construction of the book. Austen prepares the reader for Bingley's subsequent rapid departure.

To bring the argument to a close, for it has become long-winded, Bingley teases Darcy and makes light of the whole discussion. Note Darcy's reaction. He is not amused. This inability to laugh at himself is a failing that Elizabeth notices here and later (Chapter 58). Bingley's easy-going nature finds arguments unpleasant. He does not share Darcy and Elizabeth's pleasure in witty repartee.

Elizabeth feels insulted

Elizabeth's prejudice blinds her to Darcy's true feelings. She is unaware that

Pride and prejudice

his interest in her is based on growing admiration for her. She mistakenly believes he disapproves of her. Not that she cares, for she still dislikes him: 'She liked him too little to care for his approbation'.

So when he asks her to dance a reel – a country dance – Elizabeth's interpretation of Mr Darcy's request is that he wishes to insult her by inferring that she, a country bumpkin would enjoy such a dance. Her pride is hurt. Note that although Darcy is falling in love with Elizabeth, the status of her family prevents him from believing that there is any future in it.

Chapter 11

Jane, recovered, joins the rest of the company in the drawing room. Miss Bingley tries unsuccessfully to distract Mr Darcy from his reading – that is, until she persuades Elizabeth to accompany her on a walk round the room: then he looks up. In the ensuing conversation, Elizabeth reveals her pleasure in laughing at the absurdities of human behaviour. Darcy admits his dislike of being mocked and claims to conduct himself in a way that will not invite ridicule. Elizabeth teases him about this self-conscious and serious side of his character. Darcy, realising he is increasingly attracted to Elizabeth, brings the conversation to a halt, but not before he has admitted Elizabeth's prejudice against him.

'I hope I never ridicule what is wise or good. Follies and nonsense…'

Elizabeth is Austen's mouthpiece here. Consider the characters Elizabeth/Austen satirises: Mr Collins, Miss Bingley, Lady Catherine. It is not only their foolishness and 'inconsistencies' that she mocks but also their hypocrisy, incivility and lack of 'true' breeding.

Darcy and forgiveness

Notice how seriously Darcy takes himself. He makes a conscious effort not to put himself into a situation where he is open to ridicule or teasing by a 'strong understanding' such as Elizabeth's. She teases Darcy about his self-consciousness: '…Mr Darcy has no defect. He owns it himself without disguise.' She is witty too about his self-confessed defect. How true is it, though, that he cannot forgive other people's 'offences' against him? Consider his behaviour towards Elizabeth when she has rejected his proposal, and his behaviour towards Wickham after the elopement. Can it really be said that Darcy knows himself as well as he thinks? On the other hand, his behaviour towards Wickham later in the story might be seen as the actions of a man anxious to save the woman he loves from embarrassment.

Chapter 12

This chapter acts as an interlude between the sojourn at Netherfield and the arrival of Mr Collins at Longbourn. The interval at Netherfield enabled the four main characters to be better acquainted. Mr Darcy is glad of the subsequent separation as he is not yet willing to submit to his growing love for Elizabeth. The girls are welcomed home, especially by their father, as he has missed their enlivening company. Elizabeth's growing attraction for Darcy is witnessed, as is the conflict of emotions it causes within him.

Elizabeth allows her injured pride to feed her prejudice against Darcy.

In contrast, **Bingley and Jane's relationship** seems set fair.

Self-test (Questions) Chapters 1–12

Uncover the plot

Delete two of the three alternatives given, to find the correct plot. Beware possible misconceptions and muddles.

Netherfield/Longbourn/Pemberley is rented by Mr Darcy/Bingley/Wickham, starting Mr Bennet/Miss Bingley/Mrs Bennet on wedding plans. At the Meryton/Pemberley/Longbourn assembly, Mr Bingley is attracted to Elizabeth/Jane/Mary, but his friend Mr Hurst/Mr Bennet/Mr Darcy refuses to dance with Elizabeth/Jane/Lydia, and is generally disliked for his looks/pride/money. Darcy, however, finds himself 'caught' by Elizabeth's playing/playfulness/pride. When Jane/Louisa/Miss Bingley falls ill, Elizabeth stays at Netherfield: abused by Mrs Bennet/Miss Bingley/Mr Hurst, but defended by Mr Bingley/Mr Darcy/Mrs Hurst, she continues to irritate/impress/ignore Darcy, despite the embarrassing visit of her sister/father/mother, and the jealous efforts of Lydia/Miss Bingley/Charlotte Lucas to attract Darcy. Elizabeth assumes that Darcy's attention is purely critical/admiring/social, and meanwhile is delighted by Darcy's/Bingley's/Wickham's attentiveness to Jane. The sisters finally return home to Meryton/Pemberton/Longbourn.

Who? What? Where? Why? How?

1 Who is Mr Bennet's favourite daughter, and why? Who is Mrs Bennet's favourite?
2 Who have a 'very steady friendship' despite 'great opposition of character'?
3 What does Mr Darcy say to 'slight' Elizabeth at the assembly? What later episode reminds us of this?
4 What 'discoveries' does Darcy make about Elizabeth, as he becomes interested in her? Which of these is he constantly teased about by Miss Bingley?
5 What is the outcome of Mrs Bennet's plot to get Jane stranded by rain at Netherfield?
6 Where do the Bennets live, and what is the nearest town?
7 Why is Elizabeth deliberately 'playful' towards Darcy – and why is this ironic?
8 Why is Mrs Bennet so desperate to see her daughters married?
9 How do Elizabeth and Mrs Bennet variously relate the story of Darcy's rudeness?
10 How does Darcy feel when Elizabeth says she's leaving Netherfield?

Who is this?

1 Who is: an 'odd... mixture of quick parts, sarcastic humour, reserve and caprice'?
2 Who is: 'a woman of mean understanding, little information, and uncertain temper'?
3 Who is: 'good looking and gentlemanlike', with 'easy, unaffected manners'?
4 Who: 'soon drew the attention of the room by his fine, tall person, handsome features, noble mien'?
5 Who: 'was discovered to be proud, to be above his company, and above being pleased'?

6 Who: 'had a lively, playful disposition, which delighted in anything ridiculous'?
7 Who is said to be: 'a great deal too apt... to like people in general' – by whom, and why is this ironic?
8 Who were: 'very fine ladies; not deficient... in the power of being agreeable where they chose it; but proud and conceited.'?
9 Who 'had high animal spirits, and a sort of natural self-consequence'?
10 Who says: 'It has been a study of my life to avoid those weaknesses which often expose a strong understanding to ridicule'?

Familiar themes

What important theme or idea in the novel is being developed by the following lines or events?

1 'One cannot know what a man really is by the end of a fortnight', Mr Bennet says of Bingley.
2 'The rest of the evening was spent in conjecturing how soon he would return Mr Bennet's visit, and determining when they should ask him to dinner.'
3 A 'report' said that Bingley was bringing twelve ladies and seven gentlemen to the assembly. Then they 'heard' that there were six ladies and seven gentlemen. The party turns out to be five altogether.
4 Elizabeth says: 'I could easily forgive his pride, if he had not mortified mine.'
5 Darcy agrees that having uncles in Cheapside 'must very materially lessen their chance of marrying men of any consideration in the world.'

Prove it!

Back up each of the following statements from the text. (Numbers show the chapter in which they can be found)

1 Darcy's behaviour at the assembly created lasting prejudice against him. (3)
2 Charlotte Lucas represents an entirely unsentimental view of marriage. (6)
3 Darcy considers the country to offer a very limited social environment. (9)
4 Darcy is held back from loving Elizabeth only by social considerations. (10)
5 Elizabeth enjoys making fun of others – but only when they deserve it. (11)

Popping the question?

Love and marriage are an important theme in this section. Let's explore.

1 What is a 'truth universally acknowledged' at the start of the novel?
2 Contrast Charlotte Lucas' and Elizabeth Bennet's views of marriage.
3 Elizabeth is glad that Jane does not show her affection for Bingley. Why does Charlotte disagree?
4 Complete Darcy's line (end of Chapter 6) 'A lady's imagination is very rapid...
5 How does Darcy behave on Elizabeth's last day at Netherfield, and why?

Self-test (Answers) Chapters 1–12

Uncover the plot

Netherfield is rented by Mr Bingley, starting Mrs Bennet on wedding plans. At the Meryton assembly, Mr Bingley is attracted to Jane, but his friend Mr Darcy refuses to dance with Elizabeth, and is generally disliked for his pride. Darcy, however, finds himself 'caught' by Elizabeth's playfulness. When Jane falls ill, Elizabeth stays at Netherfield: abused by Miss Bingley, but defended by Mr Bingley, she continues to impress Darcy, despite the embarrassing visit of her mother, and the jealous efforts of Miss Bingley to attract Darcy. Elizabeth assumes that Darcy's attention is purely critical, and meanwhile is delighted by Bingley's attentiveness to Jane. The sisters finally return home to Longbourn.

Who? What? Where? Why? How?

1 Elizabeth: she 'has something more of quickness than her sisters.' (1) Lydia (9)
2 Darcy and Bingley (4)
3 She is not handsome enough to tempt him to dance. (3) He asks her to dance a reel at Netherfield, and she refuses, assuming it to be 'premeditated contempt' (10)
4 That her face is rendered intelligent by beautiful eyes, her figure light and pleasing, her manners attractively playful (6). Her eyes
5 Jane becomes ill. Elizabeth stays with her, which gives Darcy time to fall in love with her, but also to realise the social barriers between them, with Mrs Bennet's visit (7)
6 Longbourn, Meryton
7 Because she wants to counter his apparent contempt for her, his 'satirical eye'; ironically, it is this very playfulness that attracts Darcy, unbeknownst to her (6)
8 Because their property goes to another relative on Mr Bennet's death; they need financial security (7)
9 Elizabeth with humour. Mrs Bennet' with much bitterness of spirit and some exaggeration. (3)
10 Relieved; he is more attracted to her than he likes, and Miss Bingley is obviously sensitive to it (12)

Who is this?

1 Mr Bennet (1)
2 Mrs Bennet (2)
3 Mr Bingley (3)
4 Mr Darcy (3)
5 Mr Darcy (3)
6 Elizabeth (3)

Familiar themes

1 The inaccuracy of snap judgements about people (2)
2 The elaborate social conventions governing relationships (2)
3 The inaccuracy of 'reports and hearsay about people (3)
4 The double-edged nature of pride in the relationship between Darcy and Elizabeth (5)
5 Low social connections as a barrier to marriage (8)
7 Jane, by Elizabeth (4). Elizabeth makes the same mistake with Wickham
8 Mr Bingley's sisters: Miss Bingley and Mrs Hurst (4)
9 Lydia (9)
10 Darcy (11)

Prove it!

1 'His character was decided.'
2 'Happiness in marriage is entirely a matter of chance.'
3 'In a country neighbourhood, you move in a very confined and unvarying society.'
4 'He really believed that were it not for the inferiority of her connections, he should be in some danger.'
5 'Follies and nonsense, whims and inconsistencies do divert me, I own, and I laugh at them whenever I can.'

Popping the question?

1 'That a single man in possession of a good fortune, must be in want of a wife.' (1)
2 Charlotte thinks marriage is a matter of social and financial security; compatibility is a matter of luck. Elizabeth feels it should be based on knowledge and mutual understanding (6)
3 Because the object of her affection may also be in the dark, and she may lose him: love needs encouragement. This in fact happens to Jane (6)
4 'It jumps from admiration to love, from love to matrimony in a moment.' (6)
5 He ignores her completely, so that Elizabeth's hopes are not raised (although in fact she is unaware of his feelings!) – and perhaps also to deny his own feelings, and allay Miss Bingley's suspicions (12)

Chapter 13

Mr Bennet announces the imminent arrival of a visitor. He shows his family the letter announcing Mr Collins' arrival. Mr Collins is the distant cousin who stands to inherit the Bennet estate. He is a clergyman who has a recently acquired living on the estate of Lady Catherine de Bourgh. Saying that he would like to help the family, he hints that he is willing to marry one of the Bennet daughters.

A suitor arrives

Letters are important in this novel. As well as carrying information, they often

give a good indication of the writer's character. Mr Collins' letter reveals him to be pompous, condescending, fawning and insensitive. The Bennet family are divided as to his qualities. Mrs Bennet is favourably impressed, and optimistic that he will be advantageous to the girls; Jane thinks his motives worthy. Mr Bennet and Elizabeth see the true man.

Anyone more sensitive than Mr Collins would find it tactless of Mrs Bennet to talk about the entailment in a way that blames him for something over which he has no control.

Chapter 14

To the amusement of Mr Bennet, Mr Collins describes his luck and gratitude in being the recipient of Lady Catherine's patronage. He bathes in her reflected 'glory'. To Mr Bennet, Mr Collins is an absurd figure, who lays himself open to ridicule through his pomposity and blind deference to Lady Catherine. Significantly, Mrs Bennet accepts Mr Collins at face value and even approves of him.

Chapter 15

Mr Collins' lack of real feeling is shown in the way he rapidly switches his attentions from Jane to Elizabeth. The Bennet sisters meet Wickham for the first time and are favourably impressed by his 'gentlemanlike appearance'. Elizabeth quickly discerns that Wickham and Darcy are already acquainted, but that it is a source of embarrassment for them to meet. Mr Collins and Mrs Philips are satirised for their mutual admiration which is based on nothing deeper than exaggerated civility.

A prospect of marriage?

By way of summarising Mr Collins' character, Austen describes him as: 'a mixture of pride and obsequiousness, self-importance and humility.' His decision to marry one of the Bennet girls is based on the assumption that they are in no position (financially) to refuse him. The situation encourages his ego and makes him condescending. He obviously does not place love and compatibility high on his list of reasons for marriage.

Note Mrs Bennet's lack of discrimination and intelligence. Her sole concern is to find a husband with a fortune for her daughter. To her, it does not matter that the prospective husband is incompatible with her daughter.

A new man on the scene

Notice the way that Wickham is first described and contrasted to Mr Collins: 'His appearance was greatly in his favour; he had all the best part of beauty, a fair countenance, a good figure, and very pleasing address.' The repetition of the word 'appearance' is, however, an early-warning signal that Wickham is not necessarily the man he seems. A note of mystery is struck here, when Elizabeth notes the surprise and embarrassment of both men when Wickham and Darcy meet.

Chapter 16

At a gathering at Mrs Philip's house, Elizabeth meets Wickham again. Disarmed by his agreeable appearance and already prejudiced against Darcy, she believes what he tells her of the ill-treatment he has received from Darcy. Wickham's father had been a loyal employee of Darcy's father, who had treated the young Wickham like a second son and led him to understand that a clerical living would be his one day. When the living became vacant, Darcy broke his father's promise and refused to give it to Wickham. Wickham attributes this dishonourable behaviour to jealousy and accuses Darcy of 'malicious revenge', 'injustice' and 'inhumanity'.

Wickham, a 'gentleman'

The attractiveness of Wickham is increased by the ease of his conversation, which contrasts with the pedestrian nature of Mr Collins' talk. He cunningly evokes Elizabeth's curiosity by the use of the emotive word 'scandalous'. Wickham does not strike her as indiscreet in relating this story to a comparative stranger. It shows how much Elizabeth dislikes Darcy that she is willing to believe Wickham's story. This makes her suspend her usual scepticism and judgement.

Wickham implies that he has not bought the matter out in public because of his own sense of honour. Elizabeth finds Wickham's story plausible because his manner is attractive and open: the opposite of Darcy's.

Wickham on Darcy

Elizabeth cannot believe that a gentleman such as Darcy could break his father's promise. Surely his pride would make him behave honestly. However, Wickham suggests that other 'impulses', such as jealousy and hatred, have characterised Darcy's behaviour towards him.

Look how Wickham views Darcy's actions. He admits that Darcy acts generously towards his tenants and the poor, and lovingly towards his sister (things which Elizabeth later finds to be true when she visits Pemberley), but this he also attributes to pride: 'It has connected him nearer with virtue...'.

To the list of Darcy's faults, Wickham now adds hypocrisy. When Elizabeth asks how an agreeable man such as Bingley can like such a bad character, Wickham says that Darcy changes his behaviour to suit his company.

Chapter 17

Jane, having heard Wickham's story from Elizabeth, refuses to condemn Darcy, suggesting that the full account is not yet known. Elizabeth, however, is convinced that it is true. The Bingleys invite the Bennets to a ball at Netherfield. Elizabeth is looking forward to dancing with Wickham, but Mr Collins informs her of his intention to dance with her. She begins to realise that it is she who has been singled out as his prospective wife.

Jane defends Darcy

Jane, wanting to think well of Darcy, suggests that perhaps the full story has not yet been told. For once, her desire to see good in everyone is justified.

Balls and dancing were the major social activity of people of this class, especially when in the country. The ball would provide the main topic of conversation for a week beforehand and for days afterwards.

Chapter 18

At the ball, Elizabeth is disappointed at Wickham's absence and finds she must dance with Mr Collins, a cause of 'shame and misery'. Mr Darcy takes her by surprise and engages her to dance. Unable to learn much from him about Mr Wickham, she continues to believe Wickham's story, despite contrary evidence from Miss Bingley and Jane. She is ashamed by the behaviour of certain members of her family: Mr Collins obsequiously introduces himself to Darcy; her mother talks loudly about her hopes that Jane will marry Bingley; Mary sings too many songs; and her father is publicly sarcastic. The final embarrassment is Mrs Bennet's ploy to be the last to leave, when it is obvious to Elizabeth that they have overstayed their welcome.

Elizabeth assesses Darcy's character

The dance, one of the chief ways a couple could talk fairly intimately in private, could be a source of misery with a boring partner. Contrast Elizabeth's dances with Mr Collins and with Mr Darcy. Although she would

Elizabeth Bennet

never admit to enjoying it, her conversation with Darcy is animated. Darcy is reluctanct to give his side of the story. Blinded by prejudice, Elizabeth does not see this as virtuous. Austen uses picture imagery to describe character. Notice the use of the words 'illustration', 'sketch', and 'likeness' in Elizabeth's assessment of Darcy's character.

Sir William and Mrs Bennet talk of marriage

Darcy is alarmed by Sir William Lucas' assumption that Jane and Bingley are to be married. As he later explains, he believes Jane is indifferent to Bingley and is therefore alarmed that his friend might be rushing into a marriage he will later regret. Notice Mrs Bennet's indiscretion in discussing the possibility of marriage between Jane and Bingley. Ironically, she causes the disruption

Love and marriage

in their relationship because Darcy, alarmed by the schemes he overhears, persuades his friend to leave quickly for London.

Charlotte's attitude towards marriage is shown in her remarks to Elizabeth about Darcy. To her, Darcy should not be dismissed in favour of Wickham because the former is 'a man ten times his consequence'. In other words, it is highly significant to her that Darcy is by far the richer of the two.

Prejudiced opinion

Pride and prejudice

'It is particularly incumbent on those who never change their opinion, to be secure of judging properly at first.' Elizabeth's statement is unconsciously ironic. It is she who has *not* judged Darcy 'properly at first' and her prejudice continues to cloud her judgement. She will not believe Miss Bingley because she suspects her motives. So complete is her prejudice against Darcy and in favour of Wickham that she will not even trust Bingley's mild reaction against Wickham's character, as reported to her by Jane.

Mr Collins introduces himself

Mr Collins

Mr Collins, with his strange mixture of 'self-importance and humility', is anxious to introduce himself to Darcy because of their mutual connection – Lady Catherine is Darcy's aunt. Elizabeth, fearing that Darcy will regard it as 'impertinent freedom', tries to dissuade him. Mr Collins believes that his status as a clergyman places him 'as equal in point of dignity' to Mr Darcy. Mr Collins is so thick-skinned he does not notice the scorn with which Darcy treats him. However, Elizabeth *is* sensitive to Darcy's contempt for Mr Collins. She also has pride, pride that is wounded by the behaviour of her relations, because subconsciously she cares about what Darcy thinks.

Chapter 19

Mr Collins declares his intention to propose to Elizabeth and Mrs Bennet gives her consent. His proposal includes a list of reasons why he needs to marry. At first he will not accept Elizabeth's refusal and reminds her that in her economic position she might not receive as good an offer again.

Mr Collins proposes

In listing the reasons why he should marry, Mr Collins is insensitive to Elizabeth's feelings, making no mention of love, affection, respect or compatibility. It is a tribute to Elizabeth's strength of character that she manages to remain civil in her reply to him.

Mr Collins

Chapter 20

Mrs Bennet, shocked at Elizabeth's refusal to marry Mr Collins, seeks her husband's support. He is against the marriage. In his usual verbose and pompous way, Mr Collins gives up his pursuit of Elizabeth.

Behind Mrs Bennet's comical attempts to force Elizabeth to marry there are real fears based on economic facts: Elizabeth will inherit no money of her own when her father dies.

Love and marriage

Chapter 21

Mr Collins treats the matter of Elizabeth's refusal with 'resentful silence'. Elizabeth again meets Wickham, who explains that he stayed away from the ball because he did not want to meet Darcy. Elizabeth is flattered by his attention. A letter from Caroline Bingley reports that the Netherfield party have departed for London for the winter. Jane takes the letter at face value and is hurt by the suggestion that Bingley is interested in Darcy's sister. Elizabeth, though surprised by the suddenness of the departure, remains confident of Bingley's affection for Jane. She perceives that the 'relationship' between Bingley and Georgiana Darcy has more to do with Miss Bingley's wishes than his own.

A letter from Caroline Bingley

Jane Bennet

Caroline Bingley's letter shows the writer's unkind and malicious character, as it is intended to hurt the recipient. It also closes one phase of the novel as Bingley and Jane are now separated. The two sisters differ in their responses to the letter. Jane's good nature will not accept that Miss Bingley's motives can be anything but worthy. Elizabeth, more perceptive, suspects that malice and self-interest have driven Miss Bingley to write what is little more than wishful thinking on her part.

Misreading Mr Bingley's character

Mr Bingley

Neither Jane nor Elizabeth realise just how compliant Bingley is. Jane maintains 'he is his own master' (Chapter 21) and Elizabeth is confident that it would be difficult to 'influence a young man so totally independent of everyone'.

Chapter 22

Charlotte Lucas entertains Mr Collins and, as she had hoped, he is not long in proposing to her. She accepts because he offers her financial security – a basis for marriage which Elizabeth could not accept, and which upsets her for her friend's sake.

Charlotte accepts a proposal

Love and marriage

Elizabeth Bennet

The reasons for Charlotte's acceptance of Mr Collins are purely economic. Notice Austen's irony in describing the effects of the news on the Lucas family: Sir William and Lady Lucas work out how long Mr Bennet has to live; the younger girls look forward to 'coming out'.

Charlotte knows Mr Collins' faults and admits that his company is 'irksome', but in marrying him she is gaining something she prizes above happiness: financial security and comfort. Marriage 'was the only honourable provision…' for someone in her situation, and she regards herself as lucky.

Elizabeth is shocked at what she regards as Charlotte's mercenary motives for marrying; this, plus her conviction that Charlotte could not possibly be happy with a man like Mr Collins, makes her unhappy.

Chapter 23

Sir William Lucas breaks the news of his daughter's engagement to the Bennet family. Relations between the two families become strained. Mrs Bennet does not welcome the news that Mr Collins is to pay them another visit. Elizabeth is worried at the continued silence from Bingley.

Each member of the Bennet family reacts to the news of Charlotte's engagement: Mrs Bennet rants and raves; Mr Bennet is cynical; Jane wishes them well; Kitty and Lydia are uninterested in it except for its gossip value.

Mrs Bennet's obsession with getting her daughters married brings out the worst in her character. Holding Sir William and Lady Lucas responsible for their daughter's behaviour, she behaves rudely to them and, in continually reminding Jane of Bingley's absence, shows complete insensitivity for her feelings.

Chapter 24

News is received that the Bingleys are to stay in London for the winter. Jane is upset. Elizabeth reveals her high ideals of marriage and criticises her friend Charlotte for her prudent views. It is left to Mr Wickham to cheer the family up.

Judging by appearances

One of Elizabeth's most endearing qualities is her loyalty and regard for Jane. She is the more astute of the two, and plays a protective role towards her more naive, trusting sister. Here she is concerned about the effect Bingley's scheming sisters will have on Jane's happiness. Elizabeth's disappointment at the behaviour of Bingley and Charlotte comes from her growing realisation that it is unwise to judge people by appearance alone. Ironically, she has not yet realised that this might also apply to her opinion of Darcy and Wickham.

Views on marriage

Love and marriage

Jane tries, in her usual understanding way, to explain the practical issues which persuaded Charlotte to accept Mr Collins. She points out that Charlotte is 'prudent' and the match 'eligible'. Elizabeth takes issue with this view and with the language Jane uses: 'You shall not…persuade yourself or me, that selfishness is prudence, and insensibility of danger, security for happiness'.

A matter of judgement

When they discuss Bingley's absence, Elizabeth is the more astute, while Jane prefers to believe that she was mistaken about Bingley's feelings, rather than accept that his sisters have persuaded him of Miss Darcy's superiority.

Jane Bennet

Chapter 25

Mr and Mrs Gardiner arrive, a sensible, lively and intelligent couple. They invite Jane to stay with them in London. Mrs Gardiner joins the general prejudice against Darcy.

A balance to Mr and Mrs Bennet

The Gardiners represent the sensible side of Mrs Bennet's family and their

Love and marriage

marriage contrasts to Mr and Mrs Bennet's. In Mrs Gardiner's comment is revealed Austen's condemnation of romantic love as being too fragile a basis for marriage – ' "violently in love" is so hackneyed, so doubtful, so indefinite'. But sensible as she is, she is still herself subject to the pressures of her friends. Although she cannot remember Darcy's character well, she has heard that he is 'a very proud ill-natured boy'.

Chapter 26

Mrs Gardiner warns Elizabeth against Wickham because of his lack of fortune. Charlotte and Mr Collins are married. Jane meets Miss Bingley in London but does not learn of Bingley's whereabouts. Wickham turns his attention to Miss King, a woman of some wealth.

Chapter 27

Elizabeth, en route to see Charlotte, stops off to see Jane and the Gardiners in London. The Gardiners, seeing Elizabeth low spirits, suggest she visits the Lakes with them in the summer.

Mrs Gardiner and Elizabeth discuss Wickham's motives for proposing marriage to Miss King. Elizabeth is inclined to be forgiving of him, applauding his 'rational' motives: later, she condemns him as 'mercenary' – once she knows more of his character.

Love and marriage

A change of scene: time passes

Notice how carefully the novel is planned. Elizabeth's mood is low and January and February pass. The relationship between Jane and Bingley seems to be over; the suspense as to whom Mr Collins will marry has gone; Wickham has lost interest in Elizabeth; general opinion of Darcy's low character is established.

Wickham's accusations confirm Elizabeth's prejudice against Darcy.

Mr Collins' proposal to Elizabeth and his proposal to and acceptance by Charlotte together with her reasons for marrying him, explore aspects of the theme of love and marriage.

Self-test (Questions) Chapters 13–27

Uncover the plot

Delete two of the three alternatives given, to find the correct plot. Beware possible misconceptions and muddles.

Mr Gardiner/Philips/Collins visits, intending to disinherit/marry/endow one of the Bennet daughters. A new arrival – Mr Denny/Wickham/Lucas – attracts Elizabeth. At dinner with the Philips/Gardiners/Bingleys, he tells of his advancement/ill-usage/dismissal by Darcy/Bingley/Collins. At a ball, Elizabeth is outraged. At Rosings/Meryton/Netherfield, she is embarrassed/delighted/ignored by her family, but happy for Jane/Mrs Bennet/Charlotte. Mr Collins proposes to Jane/Lydia/Elizabeth, with the approval of Mr Bennet/Lady Catherine/Mrs Bennet, but has more success with Charlotte/Mary/Caroline. The Bingleys/Gardiners/Lucases leave for London/Hunsford/Hertfordshire. Mr Gardiner – Mrs Bennet's/Mrs Hurst's/Mrs Philip's brother – and his wife invite Elizabeth/Jane/Lydia to London, where even she realises that Caroline/Georgiana/Darcy is keeping Bingley from her. Meanwhile, Wickham/Darcy/Collins transfers his attentions from Elizabeth to Miss Bingley/De Bourgh/King; Elizabeth sets off for Hunsford/Netherfield/Pemberley.

Who? What? Where? Why? How?

1 Who is Mr Collins's patroness – and what do we learn later about her connection to events?
2 Who, according to Miss Bingley, is Mr Bingley going to marry?
3 What various events cause Elizabeth embarrassment at the Netherfield ball?
4 What warnings about Wickham are given by (a) Miss Bingley, (b) Darcy and (c) Mrs Gardiner?
5 What, according to Wickham, are Darcy's good qualities?
6 Where do Jane and Elizabeth travel, or plan to travel, in these chapters?
7 Why, according to Wickham, is there conflict between him and Darcy?
8 Why does Mr Collins say he wishes to marry?
9 How, according to Elizabeth, are the Bingley sisters trying to separate Bingley and Jane?
10 How do the Lucases and Bennets react to Charlotte's engagement to Mr Collins?

Who is this?

1 Who is: 'a conceited, pompous, narrow-minded, silly man'?
2 Who 'had all the best part of beauty, a fine countenance, a good figure, and very pleasing address'?
3 Of whom is it said that: 'almost all his actions may be traced to pride'?
4 Who is 'an amiable, intelligent, elegant woman'?
5 Who says: "Let me take it in the best light...."?
6 Who says: 'Your sister is crossed in love, I find. I congratulate her.'?
7 Who says: 'Nobody takes part with me, I am cruelly used, nobody feels for my poor nerves'?

8 Of whom is it said: "Without thinking highly either of men or of matrimony, marriage had always been her object"?
9 Who shows 'easiness of temper... want of proper resolution'?
10 Who 'was a sensible, gentlemanlike man, greatly superior to his sister as well by nature as education'?

Familiar themes

What important theme or idea in the novel is being developed by the following lines or events?

1 At the ball, Elizabeth searches for Wickham, is embarrassed by Mr Collins, talks with Darcy and watches Jane with Bingley. (18)
2 Mr Collins writes to Mr Bennet; (13) Miss Bingley writes to Jane; (21) Jane and Charlotte write to Elizabeth (26).
3 Mr Collins refuses to accept that Elizabeth does not want to marry him. (19)
4 Wickham acknowledges Darcy's better qualities to Elizabeth, attributing them to a single source. (16)
5 'Miss Lucas... accepted him solely from the pure and disinterested desire of an establishment. (22)

Open quotes

Identify and complete the following quotations. (Numbers show the chapter in which they can be found)

1 Wickham is a very plausible character. (16)
2 Elizabeth has made up her mind to hate Darcy. (18)
3 Wickham's story confirms prejudice against Darcy. (24)
4 Mrs Gardiner does not believe in romantic fancies. (25)
5 Elizabeth grows cynical about suitors' motives. (27)

Prejudicial terms?

Several aspects of the theme of prejudice are brought out in the novel. Let's explore.

1 Of whom is it said 'His appearance was greatly in his favour' (15) and 'There was truth in his looks (17)? Who is said to be seen 'only as he chuses to be seen' (16)? Why is this ironic?
2 Who says: 'I have known him too long and too well to be a fair judge' (16) and why is this ironic?
3 Whom does Elizabeth 'honour' for his reticence about the Wickham/Darcy feud? Why is this ironic?
4 Who says, to whom: 'It is particularly incumbent on those who never change their opinion, to be secure of judging properly at first' (18)? Why is this ironic?
5 What events begin to convince Elizabeth of 'the little dependence that can be placed on the appearance of either merit or sense' (24)?

Uncover the plot

Mr Collins visits, intending to marry one of the Bennet daughters. A new arrival – Mr Wickham – attracts Elizabeth. At dinner with the Philips, he tells of his ill-usage by Darcy. Elizabeth is outraged. At a ball at Netherfield, she is embarrassed by her family, but happy for Jane. Mr Collins proposes to Elizabeth, with the approval of Mrs Bennet, but has more success with Charlotte. The Bingleys leave for London. Mr Gardiner – Mrs Bennet's brother – and his wife invite Jane to London, where even she realises that Caroline is keeping Bingley from her. Meanwhile, Wickham transfers his attentions from Elizabeth to Miss King: Elizabeth sets off for Hunsford.

Who? What? Where? Why? How?

1. Lady Catherine de Bourgh (13), who turns out to be Darcy's aunt (16)
2. Georgina Darcy, Darcy's sister (21), (24)
3. Mr Collin's dancing, and introduction to Darcy, Mrs Bennet's plans for Jane's wedding, and insults to Darcy. Mary's singing. Mr Collin's sermon on the duties of clergy. Mrs Bennet's ploy to stay late (18)
4. (a) His accusations against Darcy are false (18) (b) Mr Collin makes friends, but may not keep them (18) (c) He may be mercenary (27) All true!
5. Generosity and hospitality (family pride). Kindness to his sister (brotherly pride). Ability, conversation. Just, sincere, rational, honourable and agreeable – with rich people (16)
6. Jane visits the Gardiners in London (25). Elizabeth visits London on the way to see Charlotte at Hunsford, with further plans to spend summer at the Lakes with the Gardiners (27)
7. Darcy has robbed Wickham of a living bequeathed to him by Darcy's father; Wickham attributes this to jealousy of old Mr Darcy's affection for him, and his own outspoken opinion of Darcy (16)
8. 1: Clergy must set an example; 2: It will add to his happiness; 3: Lady Catherine recommends it (19)
9. Keeping Bingley in London, and telling Jane that he is to marry Georgiana Darcy (21)
10. The Lucases start planning to spend the Bennet inheritance. Elizabeth is disappointed in Charlotte. Mrs Bennet is outraged. Mr Bennet enjoys the foolishness. Jane is charitable (23)

Who is this?

1. Mr Collins (24)
2. Wickham (15)
3. Darcy (16)
4. Mrs Gardiner (25)
5. Jane (24)
6. Mr Bennet (24)
7. Mrs Bennet (19)
8. Charlotte Lucas (22)
9. Bingley (24)
10. Mr Gardiner (25)

Familiar themes

1. Dancing, as an opportunity to pursue a relationship, have a private conversation, show 'interest'
2. Letters as a vital means of communication. The plot later hinges on a letter from Darcy to Elizabeth
3. Proposals (of which this is the first of several), their social conventions, and potential for misreading others' feelings
4. Pride
5. Financial security as a legitimate motive for marriage for a woman

Open quotes

1. 'Whatever he said, was said well. Whatever he did, done gracefully.'
2. 'To find a man agreeable whom one is determined to hate! Do not wish me such an evil!'
3. 'Everybody was pleased to think how much they had always disliked Mr Darcy before they had known anything of the matter!'
4. 'But that expression of "violently in love" is so hackneyed, so doubtful, so indefinite!'
5. 'What is the difference, in matrimonial affairs, between the mercenary and the prudent motive?'

Prejudicial terms?

1. Wickham. Darcy (described by Wickham). It is Wickham whose appearance is deceptive
2. Wickham, of Darcy. Mainly, it is too short an acquaintance that leads to poor judgement
3. Wickham – who says he will not expose Darcy for the sake of his father (having just done so!) In fact, it is the despised Darcy who refuses to discuss the matter
4. Elizabeth to Darcy. It is she who is misjudging him – and it will take a lot to change her opinion
5. Bingley's leaving Hertfordshire (implied), and Charlotte's marriage to Mr Collins

Chapter 28

Elizabeth continues her journey to Hunsford to visit Charlotte, who seems contented and unaffected by her marriage to Mr Collins. Miss de Bourgh stops briefly outside the parsonage. Elizabeth is not impressed by her appearance and is faintly pleased that she will do quite well as Mr Darcy's wife.

The Collins household

Note again how Jane Austen satirises Mr Collins with his repetition of the words 'humble abode'. Note too Elizabeth's sceptical assessment of the Collins household. She senses that Mr Collins is trying to show her what grand things she lost by refusing his proposal, and that Charlotte, although cheerful, ensures her own happiness by contriving to put as much distance as she can between herself and Mr Collins.

How does Mr Collins assess the value of surroundings and nature? Everything is quantified and numbered rather than appreciated for its own sake. Austen mocks his lack of sensitivity to beauty: 'every view was pointed out with a minuteness which left beauty entirely behind.' Look at Chapter 29 to see how he does the same to Rosings.

Chapter 29

At Rosings, Lady Catherine de Bourgh is shown to be haughty and bossy. Everyone except Elizabeth is in awe of her. Elizabeth stands up to her and senses she might be the first person ever to have done so.

Lady Catherine de Bourgh

Unlike the Lucases, Elizabeth is not apprehensive about meeting Lady Catherine. Elizabeth is not in awe of her, as she attaches little importance to rank for its own sake.

Notice how Austen uses dialogue to develop a point she has made about character. Lady Catherine's questions about Elizabeth's family *are* impertinent, despite her elevated rank. Austen deflates Lady Catherine's bossy character with: 'The party then gathered round the fire to hear Lady Catherine determine what weather they were to have on the morrow.'

Chapter 30

Elizabeth stays on at Hunsford. Two weeks pass and they learn that Mr Darcy and his cousin Colonel Fitzwilliam have come to stay with their aunt at Rosings. The two men come to pay their compliments to the Collinses and Elizabeth.

We are given more details of Lady Catherine's activities as mistress of a great estate: bossy, dictatorial and patronising, her behaviour contrasts with what we learn of Mr Darcy's behaviour as master of Pemberley in Chapter 43.

Chapter 31

Elizabeth enjoys Colonel Fitzwilliam's company, a fact that Darcy notices. His aunt's arrogance to Elizabeth embarrasses Darcy. It is apparent to Charlotte that a bond is growing between Darcy and Elizabeth, although she still fails to sense this.

Darcy becomes uneasy

Elizabeth finds Colonel Fitzwilliam an interesting, knowledgeable person to talk to. He is unlike his cousin in every way, easy in company, with a pleasant conversational manner. Darcy notices their mutual attraction and is jealous.

Darcy's embarrassment

Notice the clever use of contrast again. Darcy was offended by the lack of

Mr Darcy

breeding shown by Elizabeth's mother: now his aunt Lady Catherine shows her lack of manners.

Elizabeth's spirit is shown when she refuses to be intimidated by Darcy when she is playing the piano. Austen uses the formal conversation of the drawing room to say so much more – Darcy's comment: 'We neither of us perform to strangers' shows that he appreciates Elizabeth's lack of pretence.

Darcy and Elizabeth on 'public performance'

As members of this society, both Darcy and Elizabeth know that they are required, to some degree, to 'perform' in public. He says that shyness holds him back; she argues that practice would improve his social skills. Both are aware that the society in which they live is formal and artificial, and this mutual understanding is apparent beneath their polite conversation.

Chapter 32

Darcy visits Hunsford alone, and finds Elizabeth there, alone. He pays several such visits to Hunsford, but Elizabeth decides this is because he has nothing better to do.

Darcy's attitude changes

Note the way Darcy draws his chair nearer to Elizabeth, a sign of his desire to get to know her better. Note also his remark: '*You* cannot have been always at Longbourn'. Impressed with the liveliness of Elizabeth's mind, he implies that the society found in the country cannot provide her with enough stimulus – more evidence of his arrogance.

Mr Darcy

Charlotte Lucas voices the reader's suspicions about Darcy's motives here and Austen gradually prepares us for Darcy's proposal. Colonel Fitzwilliam's presence also increases the tension. His outgoing, agreeable personality is a contrast to Darcy's more introverted, inscrutable manner, and leads the reader to conjecture if he is not a more suitable choice for Elizabeth.

Chapter 33

Elizabeth is surprised to find she often chances to meet Darcy when she is out walking. She, still blinded by her prejudice against him, sees no design in this. Colonel Fitzwilliam tells her that Darcy is chiefly responsible for Bingley's failure to return to Netherfield. Elizabeth's dislike for Darcy is now at its height, ironically, he chooses this moment to propose to her.

Elizabeth's prejudices confirmed

Pride and prejudice

Jane Austen creates suspense by making it quite clear to the reader that Darcy has fallen in love with Elizabeth, whilst Elizabeth remains oblivious. Fitzwilliam's function here is to provide Elizabeth with information about Darcy's part in persuading Bingley to leave Netherfield and causing her sister so much unhappiness.

Love and marriage

Colonel Fitzwilliam's phrase; 'There were some very strong objections against the lady' causes Elizabeth a great deal of pain. She is convinced that it is Darcy's 'pride and caprice', his snobbery about the Bennets' low connections, which are the substance of the 'strong objections'. *Her* pride is therefore wounded. Be aware of the importance of 'connections' in determining a marriage. Elizabeth is convinced that it is this factor and not their mother's lack of breeding that chiefly convinced Darcy to persuade Bingley against a marriage with Jane.

Chapter 34

At the height of Elizabeth's prejudice against him, Darcy arrives and proposes marriage, clearly believing that he will be accepted. Elizabeth, angered by his pompous self-assurance, is outspoken in refusing him. Darcy is stunned by her accusations and abruptly leaves.

Darcy's rejected proposal

Elizabeth re-reads Jane's letters in order to stoke the fire of her indignation towards Darcy. His declaration of love could not be more untimely and comes as a complete shock to Elizabeth who, blinded by her prejudice, has been ignorant of his affection for her.

Austen does not use direct conversation to narrate Darcy's proposal. Her

narrative therefore allows her to convey Elizabeth's feelings towards his proposal whilst he makes it. We hear the proposal through Elizabeth.

Darcy has swallowed his pride and, in proposing to Elizabeth, he is prepared to overlook Elizabeth's connections, an amazing change for a man of his position

Pride and prejudice

in society. However, his very frankness about this only insults Elizabeth's own pride and deepens her prejudice against him.

Elizabeth's denunciation of his behaviour as ungentlemanly is cutting to someone of Darcy's status and breeding. Note the importance of social opinion here. Elizabeth blames Darcy not merely because he has separated Bingley and her sister but also because he has exposed her sister to society's contempt. She also lays the serious charge that he deprived Wickham of advancement.

Chapter 35

Darcy hands Elizabeth a letter in which he seeks to explain himself on two counts: one, why he interfered in Jane and Bingley's relationship and two, his behaviour towards Wickham. The latter he explains by describing how Wickham had attempted to elope with his sister. He refers Elizabeth to Colonel Fitzwilliam if she wants corroboration of his assertions.

Darcy writes a letter

Mr Darcy

Darcy's letter to Elizabeth is a pivotal point in the novel. The fact that he feels the need to explain and justify his actions shows the esteem in which he holds Elizabeth. Her criticism of him has hurt his pride and, despite its formal tone, the letter shows his complete integrity. He honestly believes he has acted for the best and this arrogance is apparent in the letter.

Chapter 36

This chapter is the turning-point for Elizabeth in her attitude towards Darcy. Only now does she apply the 'discernment' on which she prides herself and acknowledge she was wrong about Wickham and Darcy.

'Astonishment, apprehension and even horror'

The first reading of the letter leaves Elizabeth unchanged in her prejudice and

hostility against Darcy. She still cannot condone his behaviour in helping to separate Bingley and Jane.

It is the story of Wickham which begins to crack the shell of Elizabeth's prejudice against Darcy. She realises that both versions cannot be true. Whose story is she to believe? Note the powerful emotions with which this realisation hits her: 'Astonishment, apprehension and even horror'. Look back to Chapter 16 for Wickham's account of Darcy's father's will, and to Chapter 35 for Darcy's account, and analyse how the two versions differ.

In her struggle to decide which of the two men is telling the truth, note

Pride and prejudice

how Elizabeth recognises that 'the general approbation of the neighbourhood' had formed her attitude to Wickham in the first place. With her new-found 'impartiality', she reappraises his behaviour and comes up with an entirely different view of his character. First she acknowledges his lack of good taste in talking to her, a stranger, about his private life; next she realises his absence from the Netherfield ball was due to cowardice; finally she recalls the way he slandered Darcy's character in his absence.

A new view of Darcy

Just as the letter has forced her to reappraise Wickham, so does it make her

reconsider Darcy's character. Re-reading the first part of the letter, dealing with Bingley and Jane, she feels all his assertions to be 'just'. With great emotion she realises that she has been 'blind, partial, prejudiced, absurd'.

This is the turning-point for Elizabeth in her search for self-realisation. She blames her lack of perception on her vanity, which was flattered by Wickham's attention and offended by the impoliteness of Darcy.

Putting her pride aside, she has to admit that Darcy's judgements of Jane's seeming lack of affection for Bingley and her family's gauche behaviour at the ball, are understandable.

Chapter 37

Elizabeth decides to depart for home. She admits to feelings of gratitude and respect for Darcy but has not yet learnt to like or love him. She concludes that her family's low connections stand in the way of Jane and Bingley's relationship. She fears that Lydia, 'self-willed and careless' as she is, is likely to bring shame to their household.

Although Elizabeth now has respect and gratitude for Darcy, she has not yet come to like him, as she still is offended by his proud manner. She also acknowledges, with bitterness, the shortcomings of her family. She accepts that it is her family's lack of breeding, rather than Darcy's overwhelming arrogance, that is the main cause of Jane's unhappiness.

Elizabeth's brief dispute with Lady Catherine when she announces her decision to leave Rosings finds its parallel later in the story when Elizabeth refuses to promise not to marry Darcy (Chapter 56).

Chapter 38

Elizabeth prepares to leave Hunsford, but not before Mr Collins has a chance to show her what she has missed by not marrying him. She travels to her aunt's house in London, where Jane is staying.

A happily married couple?

Mr Collins' pomposity is apparent in everything he says: his false modesty

about the parsonage – 'our humble abode' – and his self-congratulation at Lady de Bourgh's patronage, are intended to underline to Elizabeth all that she has lost by not marrying him. Ironically, Elizabeth is *more* than aware of what she has missed: 'Poor Charlotte – it was melancholy to leave her to such society!' Although Charlotte makes the best of it, Elizabeth knows she can never really be happy, married to Mr Collins.

Self-test (Questions) Chapters 28–38

Uncover the plot

Delete two of the three alternatives given, to find the correct plot. Beware possible misconceptions and muddles.

Elizabeth arrives at Hunsford/Rosings/Pemberley with the Collins/Gardiners/Lucases/ and dines at Hunsford/Rosings/Pemberley, the home of Lady Catherine/Lady Lucas/ Mrs Collins. Mr Darcy arrives with his friend/cousin/nephew Colonel Fitzwilliam/ Fitzherbert/de Bourgh, who is attracted to Elizabeth/Maria/Charlotte: Darcy himself visits often, is strangely rude/amorous/silent, and keeps 'accidentally' meeting Eliza-beth/Miss de Bourgh/Lady Catherine in the Park. Fitzwilliam/Darcy/Collins inadvert-ently discloses Darcy's part in Bingley's/Wickham's/Georgiana's departure. At the height of Elizabeth's deeply-rooted dislike/admiration/hatred of Darcy, he proposes: revolted by his tenderness/pride/formality, she rejects him and further accuses him of Jane's misery/ruin/instability and Georgiana's/Miss Bingley's/Wickham's misfor-tunes. He answers her in a long argument/letter/speech, and Elizabeth's perceptions are slowly confirmed/altered/hardened. She leaves early for Longbourn/Bromley/Pemberley.

Who? What? Where? Why? How?

1 Who accompanies Darcy to Rosings: what three functions does he have in the plot?
2 Who does Mrs Collins have her eye on for Elizabeth?
3 What aspects of the proposal roused Elizabeth to 'resentment', and what 'exasper-ated' her further?
4 What does Elizabeth charge Darcy with, to explain her rejection of him?
5 What bargain had Wickham made with Darcy, and how did he break it?
6 Where had Wickham pursued Georgiana Darcy, and with what purpose?
7 Why is Darcy 'ill-qualified to recommend himself to strangers'?
8 Why has Charlotte chosen the least comfortable parlour for her use at Hunsford?
9 How does Darcy justify his decision to separate Jane and Bingley? What does he feel bad about?
10 How does Elizabeth feel about Darcy, as she leaves Hunsford to return home?

Who is this?

1 Of whom is it said: 'Her air was not conciliating, nor was her manner of receiving them such as to make her visitors forget their inferior rank'?
2 Who 'was pale and sickly; her features, though not plain, were insignificant and she spoke very little'?
3 Who 'entered into conversation directly with the readiness and ease of a well-bred man'?
4 Who 'has a great natural modesty, with a stronger dependence on [Darcy's judgement than on his own'?
5 Who says: 'Disguise of every sort is my abhorrence'?
6 Who showed: 'vicious propensities' and 'want of principle'?
7 Who says: 'My courage always rises with every attempt to intimidate me'?
8 Who: 'contented with laughing at them, would never exert himself to restrain the wild giddiness of his youngest daughter'?
9 Who is 'self-willed and careless.... ignorant, idle and vain'?
10 Who has: 'a constant complacency in her air and manner, not often united with great sensibility'?

Familiar themes

What important theme or idea in the novel is being developed by the following lines or events?

1 'I think it would be very hard upon younger sisters, that they should not have their share of society and amusement because the elder may not have the means or inclination to marry early.' (29)
2 'Perhaps these offences might have been overlooked, had not your pride been hurt.' (34)
3 'From the very beginning... your manners... were such as to form that ground-work of disapprobation, on which succeeding events have built so immovable a dislike.' (34)
4 'She could remember no more substantial good than the general approbation of the neighbourhood.' (36)

Rank bad manners?

Good breeding does not always equate with good manners. Let's explore the theme of 'civility'.

1 Look at Chapter 28, paragraph 3. What kind of 'civility' does Mr Collins embody?
2 Mr Collins is proud of Lady Catherine's 'civility' towards him (29). What form does this civility take?
3 Elizabeth is an outspoken person. How does 'civility' modify her words (end 31, mid 38, mid 34)?
4 In what circumstances is Darcy accused of behaving in a less than 'gentleman-like manner' (34)?

Turning points

Elizabeth reads and rereads Darcy's letter in Chapter 36. Sort the following lines/ events into chronological order to illustrate the progress of her change in perception.
• She 'weighed every circumstance with what she meant to be impartiality.' • She reappraises what she knows of Darcy. • She realises 'she had been blind, partial, prejudiced, absurd.' • She recognises the discrepancies between Darcy's story and Wickham's. • She has 'a strong prejudice against everything he might say.' • She sees 'the affair.... was capable of a turn which must make him entirely blameless' • She reapraises Darcy's remarks about Jane and the Bennets. • She recognises her ignorance and bias in favour of Wickham. • She realises 'the impropriety... the indelicacy.... of Wickham's behaviour

Self-test (Answers) Chapters 28–38

Uncover the plot

Elizabeth arrives at Hunsford with the Lucases, and dines at Rosings, the home of Lady Catherine. Mr Darcy arrives with his cousin Colonel Fitzwilliam, who is attracted to Elizabeth. Darcy, himself visits often, is strangely silent, and keeps 'accidentally' meeting Elizabeth. Fitzwilliam inadvertently discloses Darcy's part in Bingley's departure. At the height of Elizabeth's deeply-rooted dislike of Darcy, he proposes: revolted by his pride, she rejects him and further accuses him of Jane's 'misery' and Wickham's misfortunes. He answers her in a long letter, and Elizabeth's perceptions are slowly altered. She leaves early for Longbourn.

Who? What? Where? Why? How?

1 Colonel Fitzwilliam (30). He makes Darcy jealous of his easy way with Elizabeth (31). He discloses Darcy's part in Bingley's departure (33). He provides confirmation of the Georgiana affair (33, 36).
2 Either Darcy, whose attention seems ambiguous, or Fitzwilliam 'the pleasantest man' (32)
3 His language: her 'inferiority', his 'degradation'. His certainty of being accepted (34)
4 An 'ungentlemanlike' manner. Ruining the happiness of Jane and Bingley and exposing both to social derision. Reducing Wickham to poverty, ruining his prospects (34)
5 He took 3,000 pounds instead of the living. Having squandered it, he demanded the living too (35)
6 Ramsgate – to persuade her to elope with him, to gain her fortune and revenge on Darcy (35)
7 According to him, because he is shy, and not dishonest enough to 'perform to strangers (31)
8 So that Mr Collins is less tempted to spend a lot of time there! (30)
9 He thought Jane was indifferent. He deplored her lack of connections (as Elizabeth thought) but also the Bennet's 'total want of propriety'. Darcy feels bad at having concealed Jane's presence in London (35)
10 Respects him, is grateful for his love, sorry for his disappointment, indignant at his manner; does not regret her refusal, or wish to see him again

Who is this?

1 Lady Catherine (29)
2 Miss De Bourgh (29)
3 Colonel Fitzwilliam (30)
4 Bingley (35)
5 Darcy (34)
6 Wickham (35)
7 Elizabeth (31)
8 Mr Bennet (37)
9 Lydia (37)
10 Jane (36)

Familiar themes

1 Importance of marriage; conventions (and economics) of bringing out daughters
2 Pride: Darcy is accusing Elizabeth of it – but is simultaneously displaying his own condescension
3 Prejudice: the strength of first impressions in forming biased opinions
4 The importance of hearsay and report as the basis of 'knowledge about others

Rank bad manners?

1 'Formal civility.' Also tiresome: note the words 'detained', 'delay', 'second time', 'ostentatious', etc.
2 'Condescension', 'self-importance', 'not conciliating', 'dictating', 'dignified impertinence'
3 'The forbearance of civility' prevents protest to Lady Catherine (31). The attempt 'to unite civility and truth' spares Mr Collins (38). She makes 'little endeavour at civility' to Darcy (34)
4 In proposing (34) referring to her 'inferiority' and loving her against his will and judgement

Turning points

- She has a strong prejudice against everything he might say. She recognises the discrepancies between Darcy's story and Wickham's. She 'weighed every circumstance with what she meant to be impartiality. She sees 'the affair... was capable of a turn which must make him entirely blameless' She recognises her ignorance and bias in favour of Wickham. She realises the impropriety... the indelicacy... the inconsistency...' of Wickham's behaviour She reappraises what she knows of Darcy. She realises 'she had been blind, partial, prejudiced, absurd'
- She reappraises Darcy's remarks about Jane and the Bennets

50

Chapter 39

On their way back to Longbourn, Jane and Elizabeth meet Lydia and Kitty. Lydia regales her sisters with tales of dances and officers. She also gives them the news that Wickham is not to marry Miss King after all.

Lydia's main preoccupation is with the soldiers at Meryton. Frivolous, superficial and vain, it is easy to see why she is her mother's favourite.

This chapter prepares us for the next event in the story: Lydia's elopement. All Elizabeth's fears, expressed at the end of Chapter 37, seem to be well founded: Lydia is incapable of thinking seriously about anything.

Chapter 40

Elizabeth tells Jane about Darcy's proposal and letter. They agree they have been taken in by appearances but decide not to let what they know of Wickham's character be generally known — with disastrous results for their own family later.

Wickham's deeds are concealed

Jane's reaction to the truth about the Wickham affair is typical of her nature.

Incapable of believing ill of anybody, she endeavours to exonerate both Darcy and Wickham.

But Elizabeth notes: 'One has got all the goodness, and the other all the appearance of it'. Again the difference between appearance and reality is highlighted. The ease with which even discerning people like Elizabeth could be deceived by appearance was a real danger in Austen's society, with its emphasis on manners and breeding, and with its strict code of public behaviour. Scoundrels such as Wickham could 'perform' well in public, and be judged on that, rather than on their true characters.

Chapter 41

Lydia is determined to follow the regiment to Brighton with Mrs Forster, the wife of the Colonel. Elizabeth tries to persuade her father to ban the trip, but he refuses. Elizabeth meets Wickham again and this time is struck by his insincerity and affectation. By hinting that her attitude towards Darcy has changed, she lets him know that she has heard Darcy's side of the story. His reaction confirms that Darcy has told the truth. They part with a 'mutual desire of never meeting again'.

Dangers ahead for Lydia and Elizabeth

Elizabeth begins to see her family through Darcy's eyes: the shallowness of her younger sisters, until now a source of amusement, begins to embarrass her. She can even see why Darcy persuaded Bingley against them!

When Elizabeth pleads with her father not to allow Lydia to go to Brighton, he responds facetiously to her suggestion that the reputation of the whole family is at stake. Only when Elizabeth implores him to look seriously at the situation does he answer more sensibly. This scene reveals Elizabeth's increasing maturity, which contrasts with the irresponsibility of her father.

A new view of Wickham

As another step towards her attachment to Darcy, Elizabeth has to untie the

threads that linked her to Wickham. The fact that he thinks he can renew his attentions towards her is only offensive to her. Now she sees those attentions as 'idle and frivolous gallantry'.

Note the skill with which Elizabeth alerts Wickham to the fact that she knows the true story. She implies this without actually saying as much. Ironically, he tries to explain the improvement in Darcy's behaviour by suggesting that Darcy has adopted the 'appearance' of correct behaviour – in fact, it is he, not Darcy, who has done this.

Chapter 42

Elizabeth finds life at home dull. She looks forward to the planned tour of the Lakes with her aunt and uncle, but at the last minute the plans are changed, and they are to visit Derbyshire, where Darcy has his home, instead.

Repenting marriage at leisure

Mr Bennet's experience of marriage has been unhappy. Austen warns against

such marriages, based on 'youth and beauty' and a semblance of 'good humour'. This observation is placed strategically in the novel, coming as it does before the elopement of Lydia and Wickham. This account of Mr Bennet's marriage explains his cynical and sarcastic attitude towards his family. However, Elizabeth feels that his contemptuous attitude towards his wife is a harmful example to his children. She does not think an unhappy marriage excuses his irresponsibility as a father.

Chapter 43

Visiting Pemberley, Darcy's home, Elizabeth meets the housekeeper who paints a fine picture of Darcy's character. A chance meeting with Darcy in the park and his civility to her aunt and uncle confuses her, and her feelings about him start to change.

A new perspective

When she sees Pemberley, Elizabeth cannot help thinking that she might

have been mistress of the beautiful house and park, but she quickly remembers that the Gardiners would never have been welcome there: her prejudice against Darcy's pride is still strong.

Another step in changing Elizabeth's prejudiced view of Darcy is the housekeeper's account of his character and behaviour. Introduced as 'respectable-looking' and 'civil', Mrs Reynolds is clearly a woman to be believed. She interprets Darcy's 'pride' as reserve: a refusal to 'rattle away like other young men'. Elizabeth is shown Darcy's portrait, which shows him smiling! Note that his status and responsibility as a landowner impresses her. She feels a 'more gentle sensation' towards him.

A fresh start for Elizabeth and Darcy

Just as her opinion of Darcy begins to mellow, Elizabeth is brought face to

face with him. Elizabeth is embarrassed in case Darcy should think she is pursuing him, but his behaviour is so different to what Elizabeth expected that, ironically, it is *he* who puts *her* at her ease. Her perception of the change in Darcy is the result of two factors: he has modified his own proud behaviour, and Elizabeth's own feelings towards him have also changed. Pride and prejudice on both sides have been softened and altered.

Again we see the importance of 'breeding' in this society. Darcy accepts the Gardiners on the basis of their evident good breeding, despite their 'trade' background. Elizabeth is surprised at Darcy's civil manner, evident consideration for her and for her aunt and uncle, and desire for her to meet his sister.

Chapter 44

Darcy brings his sister Georgiana to visit Elizabeth. Mr Bingley, who is also in the party at Pemberley, asks after Jane. Mr and Mrs Gardiner recognise that Darcy is in love with Elizabeth, whilst she admits to herself that she no longer hates him.

Bingley talks of Jane

On renewing Elizabeth's acquaintance, Bingley shows that he still holds Jane in high regard and regrets not having seen her for a long time. Elizabeth is heartened. Note the passage of time in the novel. Bingley remarks that it is more than eight months since the Netherfield ball.

Elizabeth's feelings for Darcy

Elizabeth's analysis of her feelings at the end of this chapter is typical of Austen's rational approach to love. Elizabeth no longer hates or even dislikes Darcy. His good reputation and his civil manner make her respect him. The knowledge that he still loves her after her rejection of his proposal makes her grateful towards him. Respect and gratitude are a good basis for marriage, but she is still not sure whether marrying him would be for the best.

Chapter 45

Elizabeth and the Gardiners go to Pemberley, where an awkward meeting with the Bingley sisters and Miss Darcy takes place. Miss Bingley tries to encourage Darcy to be disparaging about Elizabeth's looks, but without success.

Miss Bingley's bitchy comment: 'are not the —shire militia removed from Meryton? They must be a great loss to *your* family' backfires on her: she does not know the story about Wickham and Miss Darcy's elopement. Intending to unnerve Elizabeth, she causes pain to the Darcys. This chapter is a fine study of Miss Bingley's jealousy which 'gave no one any pain but herself'.

Chapter 46

A letter from Jane tells Elizabeth of Lydia's elopement with Wickham. Another letter tells her that the couple are not yet married. Darcy calls on her just as she receives the news and he is alarmed by her distress.

Unwelcome news

Love and marriage

Just as there seemed a real chance that the relationship between Elizabeth and Darcy could prosper, news of Lydia's elopement arrives. It is important that Darcy is present when Elizabeth receives the news. He sees her distress and it is he who will later arrange the marriage and provide the finance for the wedding settlement. Ironically, Elizabeth regrets telling him of the family's disgrace, fearing that she has lost her chance with him forever: her final misjudgement of his character.

The fear that the scandal surrounding Lydia's elopement will turn Darcy against Elizabeth crystallises her feelings for him. Ironically, again, just at the moment when all hope of marrying Darcy must be over, she realises she *could* love him – but now 'all love must be in vain'.

Chapter 47

The Gardiners and Elizabeth return to Longbourn. No news is heard of the whereabouts of Lydia and Wickham. Each member of the family reacts in a different way, and it is Mr Gardiner who shows the most common sense, making practical suggestions as to the best course of action.

Taking the blame

Elizabeth is worried about Wickham's intentions, and is doubtful that

marriage to Lydia is in his plans. Under no delusions about Wickham's character, and knowing about his attempted elopement with Georgiana Darcy, Elizabeth has no choice but to see the reality of the situation.

She blames herself for Lydia's predicament because she did not make known to her parents what she knew of Wickham's character. Mrs Bennet refuses to accept any personal responsibility for what has happened. Her concern

for her daughter extends only as far as worrying about her wedding clothes – which Lydia may buy *after* she is married! Lydia's letter to Mrs Forster shows that she is completely oblivious of the pain she is causing her family.

Chapter 48

The search for Lydia and Wickham continues. A letter from Mr Collins is full of selfishness and repellent condescension.

Mr Gardiner proves his worth

Mr Gardiner writes and informs the family of the latest moves in the search for Lydia. His responsibility and reliability is contrasted to Mr Bennet, who is: 'a most negligent and dilatory correspondent'. Notice too that it is Mr Gardiner who takes practical steps in trying to find Lydia.

A letter from Mr Collins

Mr Collins' letter speaks of his relief at not having married into the family. Selfish and sanctimonious as ever, his 'Christianity' is shown to be shallow when he recommends Mr Bennet to 'throw off the unworthy child from your affection for ever'.

Mr Bennet fails in his duty

Mr Bennet now acknowledges that he has not taken his paternal duties seriously enough. He admits to Elizabeth that he should have taken her advice and refused to let Lydia go to Brighton.

Chapter 49

Mr Gardiner writes that he has found the couple in London. The financial terms of the marriage settlement are such that the Bennets assume Mr Gardiner has been very generous to Wickham.

A financial settlement

Love and marriage

Money played an important part in marriage. Mr Bennet and Elizabeth agree that Mr Wickham would not have agreed to marry for less than £10,000: a vast sum in those days. It is essential that Lydia and Wickham should marry. Even though their chance of happiness is small and Wickham is disliked, the public disgrace of elopement without marriage was very great and would have reflected on the whole Bennet family (as shown by Mr Collins' letter).

Mrs Bennet rejoices

What is Mrs Bennet's first thought on hearing Lydia is to be married? Her simple mind is 'disturbed by no fear for her felicity, nor humbled by any remembrance of her misconduct'. Instead, she thinks only of the joy of having one daughter married, regardless of the scandalous circumstances. Note her ingratitude on hearing that Mr Gardiner has given Wickham money as part of the marriage settlement.

A thoughtful Elizabeth

Elizabeth's wisdom is apparent again here. In contrast to the inane prattling of her mother, Elizabeth assesses Lydia's situation rationally and concludes that, while by no means ideal (for she does not rate her chances of 'rational happiness or worldly prosperity' very highly), it is considerably better than it had been before.

Chapter 50

Preparations for the wedding proceed. Elizabeth now admits to herself that she and Darcy are suited, but regrets that Lydia's behaviour and the circumstances of her wedding will mean that there is no hope of their marrying.

Mr and Mrs Bennet's response to Lydia's wedding

Mr Bennet is ashamed that his brother-in-law has had to bear the expense of Lydia's marriage settlement, but glad not to have been put to too much

trouble by the affair. We learn that his irresponsibility towards his daughters extends to financial matters: he has not saved any money to support his family after his death.

Austen mocks the public response to the wedding, criticising the hypocrisy of the 'spiteful old ladies of Meryton' who, knowing Wickham's character, and knowing there is little chance of Lydia being happy, send 'good-natured wishes for her well-doing'.

But who takes the correct attitude, Mr or Mrs Bennet? He says he never wants to see his daughter in his house again because of her behaviour, whilst she forgets Lydia's misdemeanours in her joy at having a daughter married. Neither parent comes out with any credit. Given the casual way in which Mr Bennet exercises his parental duty, he must take some blame for the events, and Mrs Bennet ought to have some thought for the morality of her daughter's behaviour.

Elizabeth despairs

Elizabeth now recognises that she loves Darcy, and that their marriage 'would

Love and marriage

be to the advantage of both'. The irony is that she knows a man of his status will not wish to be associated with her family after such a scandal. Here Jane Austen describes an 'ideal' marriage, based on mutual suitability. Elizabeth would have benefited from Darcy's 'knowledge of the world', Darcy from her 'ease and liveliness'. This rational approach to marriage contrasts with Lydia and Wickham's: the latter is a marriage that Elizabeth is convinced will not work because 'passions were stronger than virtue'.

Since **Elizabeth's reappraisal of Darcy** following his letter (Chapters 35 and 36), the relationship has taken another turn. **Elizabeth** sees **Darcy** on his own ground, relaxed and civil. He has also taken to heart her criticism of his pride.

Elizabeth recognises her own growing respect, affection and love for Darcy.

Wickham and Lydia's elopement dashes her hopes of marriage to Darcy.

Self-test (Questions) Chapters 39–50

Uncover the plot

Delete two of the three alternatives given, to find the correct plot. Beware possible misconceptions and muddles.

Elizabeth tells Jane/Mr Bennet/Mrs Gardiner about Wickham; they decide to expose him/say nothing/tell Mr Bennet, even when Lydia/Kitty/Jane follows the regiment to Brighton/Ramsgate/Gretna. Elizabeth departs with the Collins/Forsters/Gardiners for Lambton/Longbourn/Hunsford in the Lake District/Hertfordshire/Derbyshire. They visit Pemberley/Rosings/Blenheim, where the housekeeper Mrs Rosings/Younge/Reynolds gives a glowing account of Wickham/Darcy/Mr Darcy Senior. Darcy himself proves unusually rude/condescending/attentive to the Gardiners. Elizabeth feels gratitude/disgust/repentence, for to pride/love/politeness... it must be attributed' – but then news comes from Jane/Mr Bennet/Mr Gardiner that Lydia has eloped with/married/got engaged to Wickham: now 'all love/gratitude/pride must be in vain'. Mr Bennet/Gardiner/Darcy sends news from Brighton/Gretna/London that Wickham will divorce/return/marry Lydia for a financial settlement. Mrs Bennet is shocked/delighted/resigned.

Who? What? Why? How?

1 Who is assumed to have paid Wickham to marry Lydia: why is this ironic?
2 Who does Darcy bring to visit Jane at Lambton – and with what effect?
3 What marriages are analysed in Chapters 42 and 50, and what contrasts are made between them?
4 What is Elizabeth's opinion of Wickham when she sees him again?
5 What factors, encountered at Pemberley, put Darcy in a different light?
6 What opposite extremes do Mr and Mrs Bennet adopt in reaction to Lydia's impending marriage?
7 Why does Mr Bennet allow Lydia to go to Brighton?
8 Why does Elizabeth blame herself for Lydia's disgrace?
9 How does Elizabeth warn Wickham that she knows the truth about Darcy?
10 How does Elizabeth misjudge Darcy's character, even after she realises she loves him?

Who is this? I

1 Of whom is it said: 'There was sense and good humour in her face, and her manners were perfectly unassuming and gentle'?
2 Who is: 'as false and deceitful, as he is insinuating'?
3 Who 'was always the sweetest-tempered, most generous-hearted boy in the world'?

Who is this? II

Identify the following people by their reaction to Lydia's elopement, in Chapters 47 and 48.

1 'I always thought they were unfit to have the charge of her; but I was over-ruled, as I always am.'
2 'The death of your daughter would have been a blessing in comparison of this.'
3 'Do not give way to useless alarm.'
4 'Let me once in my life feel how much I have been to blame... It will pass away soon enough.'
5 'I am inclined to hope, he might have been misunderstood.'

Familiar themes

What important theme or idea in the novel is being developed by the following lines or events?

1 'One has got all the goodness, and the other all the appearance of it.' (40)
2 'It was an union that must have been to the advantage of both' (50)
3 'Some call him proud... To my fancy, it is only because he does not rattle away like other young men.' (41)
4 Elizabeth 'gloried in every expression, every sentence of her uncle, which marked his intelligence, his taste, or his good manners.' (41)
5 'That they should marry, small as is their chance of happiness... we are forced to rejoice!' (49)

All a question of timing

Darcy proposed to Elizabeth just when her dislike of him reached its height. What is ironic about the timing of the following events?

1 Elizabeth and Jane decide not to expose Wickham. (40)
2 Darcy is civil and attentive to the Gardiners at Pemberley. (43)
3 Miss Bingley makes a snide, veiled reference to the Bennet's relations with Wickham. (45)
4 Elizabeth finally realises she 'could have loved' Darcy. (46)

Belles lettres?

There is a flurry of correspondence in Chapters 46–48. List the various letters, and sum up in a word or phrase what each tells you about its writer. Who has not written as expected?

59

Self-test (Answers) Chapters 39–50

Uncover the plot

Elizabeth tells Jane about Wickham; they decide to say nothing, even when Lydia follows the regiment to Brighton. Elizabeth departs with the Gardiners for Lambton in Derbyshire. They visit Pemberley, where the housekeeper Mrs Reynolds gives a glowing account of Darcy. Darcy himself proves unusually attentive to the Gardiners; Elizabeth feels gratitude, for 'to love ... it must be attributed' – but then news comes from Jane that Lydia has eloped with Wickham: now 'all love must be in vain.' Mr Gardiner sends news from London that Wickham will marry Lydia for a financial settlement. Mrs Bennet is delighted.

Who? What? Why? How?

1 Mr Gardiner (49) – a final underestimation of Darcy, who in fact arranged everything

2 Georgiana Darcy and Bingley (44). This disproves Wickham's reports of her pride, and gives Elizabeth hope for Jane – even less to hold against Darcy

3 The Bennets: 'respect, esteem and confidence had vanished forever' (42). Lydia and Wickham: 'only brought together because their passions were stronger than their virtue' (50). Potentially, Elizabeth and Darcy: an union that must have been to the advantage of both.' (50)

4 She finds in his gentleness 'an affection and a sameness' and his gallantry 'idle and frivolous' (41)

5 The beauty of the estate, his stature as landowner, his housekeeper's good opinion, his smiling portrait, his civility to the Gardiners (43)

6 He rejects her completely. She is overjoyed and oblivious to any wrongdoing (50)

7 To let her expose herself without 'expense or inconvenience to her family'! He says she will give them no peace, will be in little danger, may learn humility, and couldn't get worse!

8 She has decided not to disclose Wickham's past history (40)

9 She indicates that 'From knowing him better, his disposition was better understood' (41)

10 She thinks he despises her, at the news of Lydia's disgrace: in fact he is moved by her distress (46)

Who is this? I

1 Georgiana Darcy (44)
2 Wickham (47)
3 Darcy (43)

Who is this? II

1 Mrs Bennet (47)
2 Mr Collins (48)
3 Mr Gardiner (47)
4 Mr Bennet (48)
5 Jane (47)

Familiar themes

1 Appearance and reality. A great quote to sum up Elizabeth's mistake!

2 Marriage based on compatibility. (Find the quote and read on: useful lines!)

3 'Pride' seen without 'prejudice'

4 Good 'breeding' in low rank: contrast Lady Catherine! Darcy's recognition of this also does him credit

5 Marriage was essential in such circumstances to prevent the ruin of a woman's reputation

All a question of timing

1 Immediately afterwards, Lydia leaves for Brighton, whence she will elope with Wickham (41)

2 Elizabeth has just tried to remind herself that Darcy does not approve of her connections (41)

3 Wickham is about to cause another scandal. Added irony is created by the presence of Georgiana, his previous victim – only Miss Bingley is unaware of this fact

4 Just as Lydia's elopement makes it impossible. The same happens in Chapter 50: find the lines 'She became jealous of his esteem, when she could no longer hope to be benefited by it ...'

Belles lettres?

Jane writes twice to Elizabeth (46): naive (believing the best of Wickham's intentions)

Lydia writes to Harriet Forster (47): frivolous and 'thoughtless'

Mr Gardiner writes various letters to Mrs Gardiner (48): practical, sensible, considerate

Mr Collins writes to Mr Bennet (48): pompous, sanctimonious, hypocritical

Mr Bennet, contrary to expectation, writes nothing: 'a most negligent and dilatory correspondent' (48)

Darcy fails to write to Elizabeth (48)

Chapter 51

Lydia and Wickham, now married, return to Longbourn. Lydia lets it slip to Elizabeth that Darcy was at the wedding, and Elizabeth writes a letter to her aunt Gardiner to find out why.

Lydia returns

Elizabeth, imagining how she would feel in Lydia's position, looks for signs of shame and embarrassment when Lydia returns to Longbourn. She is shocked to find no such signs. Lydia remains herself – 'untamed, unabashed, wild, noisy, fearless'. However, Wickham has the grace to look shamefaced.

Lydia's insensitivity to the feelings and efforts of those who brought about her 'honourable' marriage is apparent in her attitude that it would be 'fun' to be married. Her behaviour is as thoughtless and insensitive as her mother's. Look at the way she lets William Goulding know she is married, and the way she speaks to Jane when the family goes to dinner.

Chapter 52

Mrs Gardiner's reply to Elizabeth's letter reveals the extent of Darcy's involvement in Lydia's marriage. Talking to Wickham, Elizabeth is more open about her knowledge of his past – so much so, that they never discuss the subject again.

Darcy's good deed

The letter from Mrs Gardiner describes how far the Bennet family are  indebted to Darcy. Mrs Gardiner says that Darcy acted out of a sense of duty because he was aware that Wickham's character was not generally known. But she also believes he did it for another reason – for Elizabeth's sake.

Elizabeth, conscious that Darcy's actions were prompted by his feelings for her, regrets all the 'saucy speech' and 'every ungracious sensation' she has ever directed towards him. She admits her love for him and is proud of the way he has acted. But she is still convinced that he would never tolerate Wickham as a brother-in-law.

Elizabeth reproves Wickham

In a very subtle and ironic way, Elizabeth lets Wickham know that she has  been told about his past. Wickham asks leading questions, but is not happy with her answers – although you should note that he offers no denial of Mrs Reynold's story. Note, too, the irony with which Elizabeth suggests that she knows about Wickham's planned elopement with Darcy's sister, saying that Miss Darcy 'has got over the most trying age'.

Chapter 53

Lydia and Wickham leave Longbourn. Bingley returns to Netherfield, bringing Darcy with him. They pay a visit to Longbourn.

The return of Bingley and Darcy to Netherfield

In her usual inconsistent, insensitive way, Mrs Bennet rattles on about Bingley's arrival (having first said she will not talk about it), with no consideration for Jane's feelings. The arrival of the two men at Longbourn makes for an awkward meeting. Darcy seems to have reverted to his former manner, distant, and 'serious as usual'. Elizabeth attributes his thoughtful and silent behaviour to his dislike of her mother's company.

To Elizabeth's embarrassment, Mrs Bennet dwells at length on Lydia's wedding to Wickham, whose name is an embarrassment to both Elizabeth and Darcy.

Elizabeth is filled with despair by her mother's insensitivity. Even if Bingley and Darcy are fond of Jane and herself, her mother's lack of breeding and Lydia's scandal must stand in the way of their happiness. However, she is given cause to hope that Bingley retains affection for Jane, as he renews his attentions.

Chapter 54

Bingley and Darcy dine at Longbourn. Bingley appears to be just as fond of Jane as he was the previous November. Mrs Bennet is convinced that they shall shortly be married: but Jane refuses to believe it.

The suspense about Elizabeth and Darcy's relationship is prolonged by Darcy's quiet, distant behaviour, and Elizabeth does not have the opportunity of speaking more than a few words with him.

However, everyone except Jane is sure of Bingley's affection for her. Elizabeth thinks Jane is not being honest with herself.

Chapter 55

Darcy returns to London. The engagement of Jane and Bingley is announced.

Love and marriage

An ideal marriage

The way Mrs Bennet engineers the situation so that Jane and Bingley are left alone together is comic, and does not have the desired outcome — intially. However, the next day, after seeing her father in the proper manner, Bingley proposes to Jane. Austen's ideal of marriage is again set out here. Happiness is 'rationally founded', and the marriage is likely to be a success because of the 'excellent understanding' and general similarity of feeling and taste between the two.

Mr Bennet's prediction that they will be cheated by their servants and forever spending beyond their means is a comic reflection on the generosity of the couple.

Elizabeth the spinster

Note Elizabeth's resilience of character here: even though she is despondent about her chances of marrying Darcy, she is genuinely happy for her sister, and even makes light of her own single state: 'if I have very good luck, I may meet with another Mr Collins in time.'

Chapter 56

Lady Catherine de Bourgh arrives, unannounced, at Longbourn. She tries to make Elizabeth promise that she will not marry Darcy. In a spirited defence of herself, Elizabeth refuses to give Lady Catherine any assurances of the kind: they part on uncivil terms.

A visit from Lady Catherine

Notice the scathing way Lady de Bourgh criticises the house and garden at Longbourn and how Mrs Bennet, overwhelmed by being in the presence of a lady, is civil for once.

When she and Elizabeth are alone, Lady Catherine abruptly introduces the subject of Elizabeth's engagement to Mr Darcy. Elizabeth, refusing to be intimidated by rank and already annoyed by Lady Catherine's offensive manner, refuses to answer her questions directly. If Lady Catherine had been less obnoxious, perhaps Elizabeth would have been more open.

Elizabeth's defiance shocks Lady Catherine, who makes plain her reasons for opposing a marriage between Darcy and Elizabeth: 'honour, decorum, prudence, nay, interest, forbid it' – all reasons which Darcy had declared he had overcome when he proposed to Elizabeth at Hunsford.

Elizabeth's intelligence comes through in the way she argues with Lady Catherine, turning all her accusations back to their source: 'Your ladyship has declared it to be impossible'. Notice the dignity with which she responds to this interfering woman, who does her best to intimidate her. When Lady Catherine, in desperation, reminds Elizabeth of Lydia's scandal, Elizabeth musters all her dignity and cuts the conversation dead. It is Elizabeth, not Lady Catherine, who brings the interview to a close.

Chapter 57

Elizabeth is now sure that Lady Catherine will influence Darcy and turn him away from any notion of marrying her. A letter from Mr Collins, congratulating Mr Bennet on his daughter's forthcoming marriage to Mr Darcy, causes Mr Bennet much amusement.

A worrying time

The suspense about Elizabeth and Darcy's relationship is maintained. Still unsure of his feelings, and more upset by the interview with Lady Catherine than she showed, Elizabeth is convinced she must have lost Darcy for ever.

The letter from Mr Collins only causes Elizabeth pain because she is forced to laugh with her father at the preposterous rumour about her engagement. Mr Bennet's sense of the absurd is roused by the suggestion that Darcy is interested in Elizabeth, for he thinks that she loathes him. He does not realise how hurtful he is being to his daughter as he unwittingly hits on the truth: 'did she (Lady Catherine) call to refuse her consent?'

Chapter 58

Bingley brings Darcy to Longbourn and Elizabeth thanks Darcy for his part in arranging Lydia's marriage. Her openness leads him to declare his love and propose to her: she accepts. Both admit to shedding the pride and prejudice which prevents their friendship until now.

A declaration of love – pride and prejudice overcome

Look at the way Austen handles Darcy's declaration of love. There is no physical contact between the lovers: Elizabeth does not even meet his eye whilst he declares his love. This is a rational union based on mutual suitability of mind, rather than physical passion.

Pride and prejudice

Both of them go back over the past year of their acquaintance, reliving the obstacles which they had to overcome: pride and prejudice on both sides. Each has been 'humbled' by the other, and both feel that they are to blame!

Ironically, it is Lady Catherine they have to thank for bringing them together at the end – Darcy says Elizabeth's refusal to deny their engagement 'taught (him) to hope.'

Although they have resolved all their difficulties, Elizabeth is sensitive enough to appreciate that their relationship still needs to develop. Though she realises that her witty, spirited repartee will make a good foil to his serious nature, she knows that he is not yet ready to be teased.

Chapter 59

The news of Darcy's and Elizabeth's engagement is broken and the members of the Bennet family react in different ways.

Elizabeth is understandably uneasy about her family's reaction to the news of  her engagement. Note again the emphasis on controlling feelings by rational means. Jane and Mr Bennet are astonished by the news, as they were both so sure that Elizabeth heartily disliked Darcy. Her father is touchingly worried that Elizabeth does not love Darcy and she puts his mind at rest on that score. Mrs Bennet's reaction is fulsome indeed, and she conveniently forgets how much she dislikes Darcy, in her excitement at Elizabeth's wealthy match.

Chapter 60

The news of the marriage is made public. Elizabeth writes to Mrs Gardiner to tell her the news. Mr Bennet informs Mr Collins of the forthcoming marriage. Miss Bingley sends her 'insincere' congratulations, and Miss Darcy writes to say she is delighted at the news. Darcy and Elizabeth look forward to the time when they can settle at Pemberley.

Chapter 61

All the threads of the novel are tidily drawn together. Jane and Bingley move to Derbyshire after a year at Netherfield. Kitty's character improves without the presence of Lydia and under the influence of her elder sisters. Mary, though still inclined to moralise, becomes more sociable now that she is no longer in the shadow of her more gifted elder sisters. As predicted, Wickham and Lydia's marriage turns sour and they are continually in debt. Miss Bingley, realising that it is in her interest to adopt a more civil attitude to Jane and Elizabeth, overcomes her jealousy of them. Georgiana and Elizabeth become very close and live together happily at Pemberley. Even Lady Catherine, despite her tremendous hostility to the match at first, swallows her pride and agrees to visit Pemberley eventually. The Gardiners remain close to Elizabeth and become intimate friends of Darcy.

Self-test (Questions) Chapters 51–61

Uncover the plot

Delete two of the three alternatives given, to find the correct plot. Beware possible misconceptions and muddles.

Lydia returns, repentant/unrepentant/seemingly repentant, and lets slip that Mr Bennet/Bingley/Darcy was at her wedding; Mrs Gardiner/Bennet/Goulding tells Elizabeth of Darcy's role. Elizabeth is proud/ashamed/sure of him: Mr Bingley/Wickham/Darcy moves back to Netherfield, and renews his interest in Elizabeth/Jane/Miss Bingley, who is delighted/cautious/indifferent. Mrs Bennet is grateful/ungracious/obsequious to Darcy, who seems silent/amiable/angry with Elizabeth. After much suspense, and scheming by Jane/Bingley/Mrs Bennet, Bingley and Jane are engaged. Lady Lucas/Catherine/De Bourgh/Fitzwilliam; Elizabeth refuses/agrees/hesitates to give up Darcy, though she has little further want/hope/need of his affections. A few days/weeks/months later, he proposes again, she accepts – to the concern of Mr Bennet/Mrs Bennet/Mr Collins – and they settle happily at Longbourn/Meryton/Pemberley.

Who? What? Where? Why? How?

1 Who is told by letter of Elizabeth's engagement to Darcy, and by whom?
2 Who is Mrs Younge: what part has she played in the story?
3 What has Mr Darcy done to secure Lydia's future, and why?
4 What prompts Mr Darcy's second proposal?
5 What does Elizabeth refuse to give Lady Catherine?
6 Where do Elizabeth's private conversations with Lady Catherine and Darcy take place?
7 Why, according to Elizabeth, did Darcy first fall in love with her?
8 Why had Wickham left the regiment – and what were his plans with regard to Lydia?
9 How does Elizabeth reprove Wickham this time?
10 How does Mrs Bennet react to Jane's engagement? And Elizabeth's?

Who is this?

1 Who says: 'I have not been in the habit of brooking disappointment'?
2 Who writes: 'You ought certainly to forgive them as christians, but never... allow their names to be mentioned in your hearing'?
3 Who says: 'I am only resolved to act in that manner which will, in my own opinion, constitute my happiness'?
4 Who is: 'untamed, unabashed, wild, noisy, and fearless'?
5 Who expressed himself... as sensibly and as warmly as a man violently in love can be supposed to do'?

Familiar themes

What important theme or idea in the novel is being developed by the following lines or events?

1 'Though your accusations were ill-founded.... my behaviour.... had merited the severest reproof.' (58)
2 'Elizabeth believed all his expectations of felicity to be rationally founded' (55)
3 'The Bennets were speedily pronounced to be the luckiest family in the world' (55)
4 'Her neighbours.... had only set that down, as almost certain and immediate, which she had looked forward to as possible, at some future time.' (57)
5 'For herself, she was humbled; but she was proud of him.' (52)

Engaging irony

What ironies, in the 'tying up' of Elizabeth and Darcy, are brought out by the following lines or events?

1 Elizabeth refuses to promise Lady Catherine that she will not marry Darcy. (56)
2 Lady Catherine tells Elizabeth: 'Your arts and allurements may... have made him forget what he owes to himself and to all his family.' (56)
3 Elizabeth fears that 'The advice and intreaty of so near a relation might settle every doubt' (57)
4 When Mr Collins warns Elizabeth and Darcy, Mr Bennet tells her: 'his perfect indifference, and your pointed dislike, make it so delightfully absurd!' (57)
5 Mr Bennet jokes: 'What said Lady Catherine...? Did she call to refuse her consent?' (57)

And they lived...

1 What happens to Kitty?
2 What happens to Mary?
3 Where do Jane and Bingley move to – and why?
4 How does Lydia's marriage turn out?
5 How does Elizabeth get on with Georgiana?
6 Who become special friends of the Darcys?
7 Who: (a) 'delighted in going to Pemberley'? (b) wanted to 'retain the right of visiting at Pemberley'? (c) was occasionally a visitor'? and (d) 'condescended to wait on them at Pemberley'?

Self-test (Answers) Chapters 51–61

Uncover the plot

Lydia returns, unrepentant, and lets slip that Mr Darcy was at her wedding; Mrs Gardiner tells Elizabeth of Darcy's role. Elizabeth is 'proud of him'. Mr Bingley moves back to Netherfield, and renews his interest in Jane, who is cautious. Mrs Bennet is ungracious to Darcy, who seems silent with Jane. After much suspense, and scheming by Mrs Bennet, Bingley and Jane are engaged. Lady Catherine arrives to inform Elizabeth that Darcy is engaged to Miss De Bourgh; Elizabeth refuses to give up Darcy, though she has little further hope of his affections. A few days later, he proposes again, she accepts – to the concern of Mr Bennet – and they settle happily at Pemberley.

Who? What? Where? Why? How?

1 Mrs Gardiner by Elizabeth, Lady Catherine and Georgiana by Darcy, and Mr Collins by Mr Bennet (60)
2 Georgiana's ex-governess. She allowed Wickham to seduce Georgiana. She discloses his and Lydia's whereabouts to Darcy (52)
3 Found Wickham; tried to persuade Lydia to return; consulted Mr Gardiner; paid Wickham's debts, purchased his commission and added to Lydia's dowry. Because of Elizabeth – and because he blames himself for not exposing Wickham earlier (52)
4 Renewed hope from Elizabeth's refusal to Lady Catherine, and the warmth of her thanks to him (58)
5 The assurance that she will never enter into an engagement with Darcy (56)
6 Out of doors, walking in the garden (56) or country (58, 59)
7 He was 'sick of civility', of deference, of officious attention' – and admired her 'impertinence' (60)
8 Because of debts. He did not intend to marry her, planning a more advantageous match abroad (52)
9 Quotes Mrs Reynolds criticisms; refers to Georgina's past indiscretion and his unsuitability to make sermons'; rejects his complaints about the last living (52)
10 Delighted – talks constantly (55). Struck dumb – then delighted (mainly by Darcy's wealth) (59)

Who is this?

1 Lady Catherine (56)
2 Mr Collins (57)
3 Elizabeth (56)
4 Lydia (51)
5 Darcy (58)

Familiar themes

1 Prejudice – dissolved, and now acknowledged
2 The ideal of marriage based on rational principles of compatibility
3 The importance of marrying-off children
4 Rumour and report in small communities: the shallowness of popular judgements
5 Pride. Elizabeth is humbled by the thought of her past prejudice. She is proud of Darcy – ironically, because he has overcome his pride! (He later says, gratefully, 'By you, I was properly humbled')

Engaging irony

1 She has, at this point, no expectation that she will get the chance
2 She is quite right: Darcy has already said that his love has overcome exactly such considerations (34).
3 It does – but for her, not against her. 'Lady Catherine's unjustifiable endeavours to separate us, were the means of removing all my doubts' (60)
4 He is blissfully unaware that neither Lady Catherine nor Mr Collins are mistaken!
5 This is exactly what she called for!

And they lived...

1 Kitty becomes 'less irritable, less ignorant, and less insipid' out of Lydia's company
2 Mary is obliged to 'mix' more – continues to moralise, but is no longer in her sisters' shadow
3 The Bingleys move to Derbyshire – to move away from their Meryton relations and close to the Darcys
4 Lydia and Wickham are soon indifferent to each other. They live unsettled lives, in constant debt
5 They love each other, and Georgiana is enlivened by Elizabeth
6 The Gardiners – who brought them together
7 (a) Mr Bennet (b) Miss Bingley (c) Lydia (d) Lady Catherine

■ Writing an examination essay

Take the following to heart

- *Carefully study each of the questions set on a particular text* Make sure you understand what they are asking for so that you select the one you know most about.
- *Answer the question* Obvious, isn't it? But bitter experience shows that many students fail because they do not actually answer the question that has been set.
- *Answer all the question* Again, obvious, but so many students spend all their time answering just part of a question and ignoring the rest. This prevents you gaining marks for the parts left out.

The question

1 Read and understand every word of it. If it asks you to compare (the similarities) and/or contrast (the differences) between characters or events, then that is what you must do.
2 Underline all the key words and phrases that mention characters, events and themes, and all instructions as to what to do, e.g. compare, contrast, outline, comment, give an account, write about, show how/what/where.
3 Now write a short list of the things you have to do, one item under the other. A typical question will only have between two and five items at most for you to cope with.

Planning your answer

1 Look at each of the points you have identified from the question. Think about what you are going to say about each. Much of it will be pretty obvious, but if you think of any good ideas, jot them down before you forget them.
2 Decide in what order you are going to deal with the question's major points. Number them in sequence.
3 So far you have done some concentrated, thoughtful reading and written down maybe fifteen to twenty words. You know roughly what you are going to say in response to the question and in what order – if you do not, you have time to give serious thought to trying one of the other questions.

Putting pen to paper

The first sentences are important. Try to summarise your response to the question so the examiner has some idea of how you are going to approach it. Do not say 'I am going to write about the character of Macbeth and show how evil he was' but instead write 'Macbeth was a weak–willed, vicious traitor. Totally dominated by his "fiend–like queen" he deserved the epitaph "this dead butcher" – or did he?' Jump straight into the essay, do not nibble at its extremities for a page and a half. High marks will be gained by the candidate who can show he or she has a mind engaged with the text. Your personal response is rewarded – provided you are answering the question!

As you write your essay *constantly refer back to your list of points* and make sure you are actually responding to them.

How long should it be?

There is no 'correct' length. What you must do is answer the question set, fully and sensitively in the time allowed. Allocate time to each question according to the percentage of marks awarded of it.

How much quotation or paraphrase?

Use only that which is relevant and contributes to the quality and clarity of your answer. Padding is a waste of your time and gains not a single mark.